W9-CFY-984

MORE THAN
A
COFFEE COMPANY

MORE THAN A COFFEE COMPANY

The Story of CFS Continental

JIM BOWMAN

Printed in the United States of America

First edition

First printing

Book design and typography by Claire J. Mahoney

Published by Chicago Review Press, Incorporated, Chicago

Library of Congress Cataloging-in-Publication Data

Bowman, Jim.
More than a coffee company.

1. CFS Continental (Firm) — History — 20th century.
2. Coffee trade — United States — History — 20th century.
I. Title.
HD9199.U52C473 1986 338.7'66393'0977311 86-13657
ISBN 0-914091-99-9

CONTENTS

FROM THE AUTHOR

This book could not have been written without the help of Stanley Owens. He pushed it to completion like a mule-driver, arranging and helping to conduct interviews and contributing from his vast store of recollections about CFS Continental, for whom he has labored for more than forty-five years. Finally, he became an editor of sorts, testing and working over this account until I must admit it bears his stamp as well as mine. I can hardly present this book without acknowledging his role.

PART ONE

Coffee to the Midwest

1. THE BEGINNINGS

CONTINENTAL COFFEE COMPANY, now called CFS Continental, was founded in 1915 in Chicago by Jacob Cohn, an immigrant from Lithuania who had come to this country only nine years earlier at about the age of ten. Young Cohn, only nineteen at the time, began selling coffee to restaurants from a wagon he had bought for $25 drawn by a horse he rented for $1.50 a day.

He had already worked with his older brother Harry at the Superior Tea & Coffee Company, selling coffee, tea and spices door-to-door. Harry and his sister Ida had come from the home village of Laukava with a cousin, Walter Katzoff. Harry and Walter in 1908 had formed Superior, now owned by a subsidiary of Sara Lee Corporation.

Jacob Cohn had come in the last group, with his mother and four of his five sisters. Before he worked with Harry, he worked as an employee in a garment factory, where conditions were such that he had to get permission when he wanted to go to the bathroom. He was refused once when it was fifteen minutes before lunch time. The experience stayed with him, and in later years he was careful to provide decent and humane working conditions for his own employees.

Finishing high school was out of the question. He had to help support his mother and sisters. His father had died when Jacob was young, before the family came to this country.

Here he began full-time gainful employment with very little formal education. He started Continental Coffee on March 15, 1915. One report has him selling coffee house-to-house. If he did, it was an early aberration, because restaurants and cafeterias were his prime customers.

He picked up his green (unroasted) coffee at the train station several times a week. He hauled the green coffee to a roaster and told the roaster how to blend it, watching him while he did it to be sure it was done right.

Then he put the blended and roasted coffee back in the same bags the green coffee had come in and carried it in his wagon to a storefront on Ogden Avenue on the city's West Side. There he ground it and transferred it to smaller, one-pound bags. This was something new. Others sold coffee to restaurants in bulk, in five- and ten-pound bags. Jacob Cohn sold it in the smaller bags because that way the coffee would stay fresher. He didn't know it, but he had created a marketing tool.

When he sold coffee, he tried to get an order for the following week. Perhaps most important, he cleaned the customer's coffee urn and made sure it was functioning properly. He sold "good coffee, delivered fresh and often" so that it would be drunk in the best condition possible. He wanted his coffee to taste good. It became a fortunate obsession with him.

There is a picture of him in those days as a very young man in white shoes, middling light suit, white or light tie, white shirt and a straw hat held by one hand at his side, standing, looking straight at the camera. He looks prosperous and dapper, with as clear a gaze as one could ask for.

He hired delivery men who were also salesmen, partly because the delivery man showed up every week while a salesman might not. This gave the delivery man a chance to do more selling. One of the first of these "route men" was a relative of his in Detroit, Albert Marans. The route men in their weekly visit kept restaurant shelves stocked with coffee, rotating it to keep the oldest up front, and solicited and took orders for delivery a week later. They were more than drivers, of course; they were salesmen who also checked, repaired and if need be replaced equipment.

Restaurant customers were given the route man's home phone number and told to call when they needed anything. Jacob Cohn developed the first routes. As he finished developing one, he gave it to one of his driver-salesmen and began another. The pattern would continue throughout the route-salesman era, into the early 1970s. Routes were split and new ones formed in amoeba-like progression — a seemingly never-ending process of division followed by multiplication.

By 1920 Jacob Cohn's Continental Coffee Company employed fifteen people and roasted its own coffee — 10,000 pounds a week — in a 6,000-square-foot rented plant on Ogden Avenue. A year or so later, the young company moved to bigger quarters, also rented, at 659 West Lake Street.

About this time, in 1921, Walter Belinky joined the company as a twenty-year-old cashier, bookkeeper, credit manager and stock boy all rolled into one. Mr. Belinky was later to be sales manager for Continental and to develop a reputation among salesmen for his inventiveness and command of detail.

The company had four salesmen at the time, plus three people in the office — a manager, an assistant manager and a switchboard operator. Mr. Belinky himself counted by hand urn bags and menus, which salesmen gave to customers. He also wrote advertising copy and speeches for the sales manager.

With difficulty Jacob Cohn persuaded Mr. Belinky to go selling, sending him on his first day to visit four lapsed accounts. Dropped at Milwaukee and Ashland on the city's Near Northwest Side, Mr. Belinky was told it was "as good a place to start as any." He walked forty blocks that day and got business from each of the four accounts. He spent two years then as a salesman making cold calls, then two on a route and in 1930 became general sales manager for the company.

One of the triumphs of those days was the so-called "grinder plan." Electric coffee-grinders were loaned to restaurants who were good-sized prospective coffee customers. These units were placed on the counter near the cash register so that dining customers could smell the fresh-ground coffee as they ate. The grinder used this way was a good marketing tool. The aroma alone was a big attraction. In addition, people could see how freshly the coffee was prepared. The restaurant would buy "bean" or unground coffee for use in its grinder. The grinder was loaned to the customer for use as long as he bought Continental coffee.

Not favoring the slim advice he was given on his first day, Mr. Belinky devised instructions for salesmen such as his "Selling Guide." By 1960, when he reminisced about these old days for the employee newsletter, he was spending eighty percent of his time in the field with salesmen, goading and advising them towards more effective sales efforts.

Meanwhile, another of the early Continental-connected people, Henry Koven, had begun the practice of law in a few rooms at One North La Salle Street. By April of 1923 his clients included Continental Coffee Company, which was paying him a monthly retainer of $33.33. Mr. Koven had received his law degree from Chicago's Kent College of Law, which he attended at night after arriving in Chicago from his native England. He practiced alone until after World War II, when he was joined in partnership by his son Howard, who with a successor firm, Friedman and Koven, remained Continental Coffee Company's chief counsel into the mid-1980s.

In 1925 Aaron A. Good joined the firm at 659 West Lake Street as a shipping clerk. Later he was for many years the credit manager, checking on bill payment and when necessary going after delinquent customers with alacrity and persistence. When customers failed to respond to letters or telephone calls, Mr. Good would call on them personally, not hesitating to face late-payers in person. He also became known for his letter-writing ability, winning awards offered by the Dartnell Corporation, a training company that sponsored contests in business letter writing.

The Lake Street building, like the Ontario Street building after it, was plagued with elevator problems. Breakdowns every few days would require Mr. Good to carry downstairs by hand the coffee just roasted on an upper floor.

Mr. Good had come to Chicago in 1924 and enrolled in De Paul University in a pre-law course. In Chicago he met Jacob Cohn, who said he ought to work for Continental. He moved through a succession of jobs (coffee packer, assistant office manager, etc.) to head of the credit department in 1928, protesting to Jacob Cohn his inability to express himself well in English. Mr. Cohn promoted him nonetheless. Encouraged by the promotion, Mr. Good went out and bought himself four English-translation dictionaries, one for each of the four languages he spoke besides English. He also enrolled in public speaking and English courses at Northwestern University and at La Salle Extension University, a correspondence school.

Joe Davis joined the company the same year as Aaron Good, in 1925. He was seventeen years old and came from Centerville, Iowa, where Jacob Cohn's sister, Anna Bloom, lived. The Blooms had a store there. Mr. Cohn would come out once a year or so to visit but was always on the lookout for salesmen for his coffee company. Anna Bloom's son Jack later joined Continental and became its chief food chemist and developer of its food-processing operation.

Joe Davis worked at Continental until September 30, 1980 — fifty-five years. He died of a heart attack in a doctor's office in Columbus, Ohio, in October, 1985, a few days after being interviewed for this book. Others who came from Centerville were Joe's brother Harry, Art and Nate Long, Henry Hirsch, Jack Bloom and his sister Sylvia and some cousins of Jack Bloom on his father's side, David and Sam Bloom.

Joe Davis joined the company at 659 West Lake Street,

where he also began in the second-floor shipping room. The coffee tester was a man named John McGoon, the office manager a woman named Flanagan. A third office helper, Katie McGovern, filled out what Joe Davis called "the Irish contingent." Joe filled orders and got things ready for the route men. But Jacob Cohn never kept people inside if he could help it. In six months, at eighteen, Joe was given a route of his own — Route C, from Jackson Boulevard south to 22nd Street and from Lake Michigan all the way to the western suburb of Downers Grove. It was a long, narrow strip less than two-and-a-half miles wide at its east end and dozens of miles long.

A year or so later, spotted by Jacob Cohn as a natural, Joe Davis opened up a route in Grand Rapids, Michigan, working under Al Marans, who at that time supervised sales throughout Michigan. In 1929 he went to Toledo, arriving in time for the first bank failure of the Great Depression. Driving his Model-T Ford panel truck with two windowless doors and three floor pedals (clutch, reverse and brake), he covered 1,000 miles a week all over northwestern Ohio, touching down in Toledo, Bowling Green, Lima, Sandusky and other towns.

The company had no office in Toledo, only an answering service. The freight dock of a trucking terminal served as a warehouse, where Mr. Davis would leave shipped coffee until he needed it. Some Continental drivers kept their inventory in their trucks. Overhead was kept to a minimum. Jacob Cohn believed in "very tight controls." One of the competitors in Toledo was Karavan Coffee Co., later bought by Continental.

From Toledo Mr. Davis went to Milwaukee, arriving on time for another bank emergency, the national bank holiday declared by President Roosevelt. Waking on a Saturday with the intention of going to the bank, he was informed the banks were closed. The company told him to keep what customers paid him and live on that until the banks reopened.

Back Joe Davis went to Chicago, this time to sell "allied" (non-coffee) products exclusively. He was the first to sell these products for Continental. At first these were gelatin, puddings (called "cream" desserts) and hot chocolate. Later they included salad dressings, dehydrated soup, sauces, syrups and the like. Continental began selling these items when the Gumpert company asked Continental to carry them. Joe Davis's instructions from Jacob Cohn were that if he could sell $100 a week worth of the new products, it would be enough to keep the line going.

Continental had probably ten routes going at this time, including South Bend, the first Indiana route. Joe Davis hit the road again for yet another new territory, Columbus, Ohio. Driving his Model T in winter, he was a natty salesman indeed, in derby, spats and a good warm coat with a velvet collar. He had to dress for warmth as well as style, since the Model T had no heater. As soon as heaters became available, he got one. Customers marveled at the cleanliness of his truck and at the shine he was able to give it. He cranked the engine to start it.

His first week in Columbus, he opened almost sixty new accounts. By his second week, he was selling enough to cover his salary and make a profit for the company. Continental was new in town. As in most of the small- to middle-sized cities and towns where Continental regularly did so well, the competition was entirely local. "We were hungry. They were complacent," said Mr. Davis.

Continental was the first coffee company to give restaurant owners menu papers, urn cleaners and urn bags and the first to sell them coffee-brewing equipment, which Continental sold almost at cost. "We were always a step ahead," said Mr. Davis. The company in those days was also always short on capital. Mr. Cohn's relations with the bankers were good, however. He got to know them, and they him. It was naturally a point of great importance, just as decades later it was important for Continental as a publicly held company to know and be known by analysts and others in the investment community.

Joe Davis settled in Columbus in 1932 or 1933, ending the nomad existence imposed on him by his uncanny ability to open new sales territories and trouble-shoot in ones already opened. By 1934 he was being praised in the employee newsletter, the *Continental Courier,* as a "star salesman" who was also "tall, dark, and handsome" — a winning combination, to be sure. By 1940 he was district sales manager with six routes under him, serving southern Ohio and West Virginia. Mr. Davis stayed in Columbus through his retirement in 1980 to his death in 1985.

Meanwhile, Joe Davis's brother Harry, a year older than he, made the move from Centerville, joining Continental in 1927, a year after he graduated from high school. In fact, the entire Davis family came to Chicago, their father having come on bad times in Centerville. Joe rented an apartment for them all, and Harry started work in the Continental shipping room.

It was a good place to start, because there one could learn the general routine, the various kinds of coffee and the like. The whole operation was on the top floor of a building shared with Spaulding Fibre and three other companies. That's where the coffee was roasted and packed for shipping. Harry Davis's first job was to feed the "hopper" for the roasting machine. Now retired and living in Evanston, Illinois, he can still remember the head roaster on hot summer days, dripping with sweat, his pants rolled up, overseeing the sweltering operation. The green, unroasted coffee arrived downstairs in 133-pound bags and was brought up on the elevator shared with the other companies — when the elevator was working.

After six months in the shipping room, Harry too was given a route. His was Route A, from Wacker Drive in Chicago north to suburban Evanston and west from the lake to Arlington Park race track, in what is now sometimes called "the land beyond O'Hare." He too drove a Model T, with paper stuffed in his shoes to keep his feet warm in winter, and always wore a bow tie. Later he was given Route D, for downtown (from Lake Street to Van Buren Street and Lake Michigan to Halsted Street). Because of heavy traffic in this area, deliveries began at 4 A.M. Because deliveries were so big, the salesman had the help of a delivery man who drove his own truck.

In the late '20s and '30s, when Harry Davis began his route work, the company sold a whopping ten blends of coffee — WB, Favorite, BG, Twin Cities — a light roast, the way people liked it in Minneapolis and St. Paul — and others. The company carried so many blends and grinds because competition was tough and labor was inexpensive. A coffee company did almost anything to please its customers.

Among competitors was Stewarts coffee, a heavy and generally more expensive blend. If you took an account away from Stewarts, Harry Davis recalled, it was a feather in your cap. For the Corona Cafe on Rush Street, Harry Davis had a special blend which was more expensive. Part of the Continental approach was to make a customer feel special with such special treatment. Part of this effort was to be available to him day or night for emergency service or deliveries. A late-night dropoff to a customer was not unusual.

Continental was selling coffee, tea, chocolate and spices almost exclusively. How the coffee was served made all the difference. Was the urn bag or faucet dirty? It was up to the salesman to make sure it wasn't, to see the coffee was brewed right. If there was a question of using a little more coffee to make a better cup, the salesman had an eighteen-ounce bag to go with the customary three gallons of water in the urn instead of the usual one-pound bag.

On June 3, 1927, the company was sufficiently established to have its twelfth annual employees dinner, at the Alamo Cafe in Chicago. In 1928 Continental moved out of the cramped Lake Street quarters into its own building at 371-375

Little Jack's Restaurant, 3175 West Madison Street, on Chicago's West Side in the mid-'30s – a Continental customer of long standing, famous for its cheese cakes. Coffee cups are ready to go "over the counter one by one, bright as soldiers on parade," filled with Continental coffee.

West Ontario Street — a structure of 36,000 square feet where Continental could roast over 50,000 pounds of coffee a week. Down the street, at 363 West Ontario, were offices of the Staley Sales Corporation, the corn products company which fifty-six years later was to buy Continental. Staley the neighbor was to become Staley the parent.

On January 2, 1929, Jacob Cohn was made an honorary member of the Chefs of Cuisine Association, of Chicago. Six months later, readers of "Coffee Grounds," published by Continental "in the interests of patrons and those who may become patrons," might have read this encomium for the product, perhaps written by Walter Belinky:

> When the first faint light of dawn sprays the sky with brilliant gold, and the first slow line of men begins its winding march to work, then Continental Coffee goes on duty.
>
> Over the counter one by one, bright as soldiers on parade, go the shining cups filled with the rich, sparkling golden brew. All day long the march of glowing cups keeps up; and all day long the merry march of coins returning — over the counter — into the till.
>
> Look high and low, look far and wide, and nowhere will you find a finer friend than Continental Coffee. Loyally, earnestly, in every kind of weather, Continental works for you. Unfailingly it stays on the job — building your reputation, adding to your trade. Asking little, it does much. If you want to serve good coffee — delicious coffee — day in and day out, let Continental go to work — for you.

Going to work for the restaurateur involved more than selling coffee, as we have seen; and Jacob Cohn began to feel for the operator whose urns cost him a pretty penny and often needed

Mitchell's Restaurant, 18 South Clark Street, in Chicago's Loop in the mid-'30s. Continental coffee waiting to be placed in Continental urns.

repairs. If he was doing so much for the customer, why not do more? Why not broaden the concept of service by making sturdier urns and selling them at cost to the cost-conscious restaurant owner?

In 1931, Continental did this by entering the coffee-urn manufacturing business, taking over the fourth floor at Ontario Street for this purpose. Mr. Cohn hired a virtual genius for this task, Frank Ehrenreich. The company began with a two-gallon brewer for restaurant use, with the express intent to reduce waste and gas consumption. Eventually, under Mr. Ehrenreich's direction, it developed a line of brewers and urns up to a twenty-gallon capacity.

Not long after urn-production began, the company began to offer other items for restaurant and institutional kitchens, the allied-products line (foods) which Joe Davis began selling with hopes of making $100 sales a week.

The house organ "Coffee Grounds" with its high praise for Continental coffee gave way to another magazine-style approach to the institutional food market, a roto-style picture magazine called *Good Coffee*. The January, 1932, issue (Volume 3, Number 1) led off with testimony of another sort, a letter from satisfied customer Ward B. James, manager of the posh Hotel Windermere East, in Chicago's Hyde Park area on the South Side lakefront.

Mr. James, who had switched to Continental coffee several months earlier, said he could "unhesitatingly recommend" the Continental Coffee Company to "any food establishment." Continental coffee had passed the test of the Windermere's "discriminating clientele," which made "exacting demands," Mr. James wrote.

A partial list of other Continental customers listed in the magazine gives an idea how far and with what success Continental salesmen had traveled. The list included the Wigwam Cafe, Wahoo, Nebraska; Chicago Yacht Club; Smith Cafeteria and Moderne Restaurant, South Bend; Palace Cafeteria,

Peoria; Manhattan Cafe, Des Moines; Goodyear Tire & Rubber Company (probably cafeteria), Akron; Mader's German Restaurant, Milwaukee; Kennedy Catering Company, St. Louis; Wagner's Waffle Shop, Sioux Falls; YMCA (cafeteria), Rochester, NY; Bide-a-Wee Tea Room, Newport News, Virginia, and various other eating places in Minnesota, Arkansas, Oklahoma, and Kansas.

The same issue of *Good Coffee* listed what was offered free to customers: an instruction card giving "Our Rules for Making Good Coffee," menus, urn cleaners, urn rings and sacks, gauge glasses and gauge brushes.

Products included coffee, instant chocolate (spelled "chocolat") imported from Holland, 100 packets to a carton, and tea balls or bags, Orange Pekoe (black) and Uncolored Japan (green) in cartons of 500, 250 and 100. The magazine also featured pictures of coffee being drunk all over the world — by Bedouins in Algeria, skiers in Switzerland, and the fashion elite in an Amsterdam sidewalk cafe.

On March 19 and 20, 1932, Continental held its first general sales convention. The company that had begun with one man selling from a horsedrawn cart seventeen years earlier had established itself as a coffee roaster and supplier in Chicago and the Midwest.

2. SELLING COFFEE TO THE MIDWEST

No one did as much to gain success for Continental as its salesmen. They obtained the business for the coffee and food products. Their orders flowing into Ontario Street day after day fueled the roasters and food processing operations as much as if they were electrical switches.

Leading the salesmen were five men, district sales managers, hired by Jacob Cohn to do the work he had begun ten to twenty years earlier. These were the men whom we might call "the five horsemen" of the Continental sales force who more than any others paved the way.

The first was Bernard Pippenger, who in 1925 answered an ad in a South Bend newspaper while he was laid off from Studebaker, the automaker, and started selling for Continental in that city. Aggressive, bright, soft-spoken, he did well there and in a few years went to Indianapolis, where eventually he became sales manager for all of Indiana. His territory later also included parts of Kentucky and Tennessee. He became well known in Indianapolis and he hired, trained, and helped his salesmen. Among Continental salesmen, he came to be considered the "dean" of Continental district sales managers.

Another was Merton Mack, short, stocky, aggressive, articulate, persistent. Out of Decatur, Illinois, he was sales manager for all of Illinois outside Chicago. He dressed nattily and was a walking men's clothing store. He hired salesmen just like himself, with fast comebacks to arguments people might make why they should not buy Continental coffee.

Mr. Mack worked closely with Mr. Pippenger, whom he respected and who respected him. During the war years, he had to take a route under Mr. Pippenger, who was given both states as an economy measure. He did so with a smile and when the war was over, came back again to head Illinois — a territory so big that one of his salesmen, Herschel Harvey, drove 50,000 miles a year in his truck.

Gene Irwin was another. Hired as a mechanic at Ontario Street, he was recruited by Jacob Cohn to sell, almost against his will, and ended up manager for all of Michigan outside Detroit. He opened up Michigan for Continental, while based in Lansing. A big man with big shoulders, he would let people think he was unsophisticated, just a country boy. He did not wear clothes well. He was honest through and through and communicated that by his manner.

As a mechanic, he was asked one day to drive Jacob Cohn downtown. On the way they talked, and Mr. Cohn spotted him for a salesman. He did the driving on another day, and Mr. Cohn put it to him: would he want to sell? He would not, he was very happy where he was. A few days later, a relief salesman didn't show up, and the city sales manager, Joe Katz, was about to take the route. Mr. Cohn told him no, Mr. Irwin would take it, which he did, just for that one day. When someone was needed the next day also, Mr. Irwin was again prevailed upon to go out selling. A few more days of that, and he was a mechanic no longer. Eventually he went to Lansing to be district manager.

Robert Campbell began as a route man under Mr. Pippenger in 1938, then went to Cincinnati as sales manager for Southern Ohio, Northern Kentucky and West Virginia. Tall, well built, polite and with a pleasant face and smile, he would do anything for a customer. He leaped to the defense of his own men when Chicago complained, but never made excuses for them. Also in dealing with customers, if he couldn't do something, he'd say so. He wasn't afraid to admit a problem.

The fifth of the "horsemen" was Dan Pacini. Mr. Pacini is eighty-five and still drives his car on the streets of San Francisco, where he lives. He began at Continental as a salesman in 1930 at the age of thirty, skipping the usual stint in the shipping room because of past experience.

The Crash of 1929 had cost him his home and other property and left him practically broke after nine years of hard work at two or three careers — as restaurateur, real estate salesman and salesman for a wholesale grocery outfit. He had his own restaurant for a few years, the Florentine Cafe, at 475 East 111th Street. He sold it in 1925 and went into real estate. Later he sold groceries to retail stores. In 1931 he decided to go to work for Continental. This was news to Continental, but he broke it to them gently.

He knew about Continental from two vantage points. He had used their coffee as a restaurant operator, and his brother-in-law, Gene Baldelli, worked there as head of the truck maintenance department at the plant at 371 West Ontario Street.

He'd just gotten a job selling for Reid Murdock, a Chicago grocery wholesaler, but even as he walked out of the Reid Murdock offices at Wacker Drive and La Salle Street, he had second thoughts. Why not go with Continental Coffee Company? The product was something he could believe in. His brother-in-law said it was a good place to work. And he, Dan Pacini, was hungry — hungry for success and the good things it could bring him and his family.

He walked out of Reid Murdock and right over to Ontario Street west of Orleans. The sign over the switchboard said "Information." He asked to see the sales manager, Walter Belinky. He had the name from his brother-in-law. He would talk Mr. Belinky into hiring him if it killed him.

Did he have an appointment? No, he didn't, but the lady

should tell Mr. Belinky that the gentleman was a salesman who had traveled sixteen miles to see Mr. Belinky and had something "rather important" to tell him. There was no need to mention that he had just walked six blocks from his new place of employment. The ploy worked. Mr. Belinky did see the gentleman from sixteen miles away, who told him he had decided to work for Continental Coffee Company.

"I'm glad you feel that way," said Mr. Belinky. "But there are no openings." Continental hired high-school graduates whom they put in the shipping room to learn the ropes and then sent out on the street if they looked promising. Mr. Pacini begged to differ with the sales manager. There was no such thing as an organization without an opening for a good salesman, he said. "I am more convinced than ever that I want to work for you," he told Mr. Belinky.

He gave his references, detailed his experience and as a clincher laid out his personal plans to do well and achieve great things for himself and his family. He said he wanted his family to have a good education and the finer things of life.

The pitch made sense to the sales manager, who could tell desire when he saw it. "I'll do it free, to prove I can sell," added Mr. Pacini, meaning he would sell on commission alone without salary. The company had nothing to lose. Mr. Pacini was hired on a commission basis and sent into the field with coffee samples and with instructions to call his orders into Mr. Belinky directly.

In his first few calls, he found the going tough. Restaurant owners liked the coffee they were using and saw no reason to change. There was something personal about the coffee a restaurant served. Changing your brand of coffee was a little like getting a divorce; it took a lot of thought and a strong push. The grass had to look a lot greener, else why change?

Mr. Pacini, a former restaurant-owner, put himself in the place of his prospective customers and decided to do what in fact other Continental salesmen were doing — brew coffee on the spot and serve it to the prospective customers. Let them decide for themselves if Continental was as good as he claimed it was. Give a blind taste test and let the chips fall where they may.

It worked. Within a week or so, he was pulling in two or three new accounts a day, calling them into Walter Belinky, who apparently began to think he had a live one in this Mr. Pacini. In a few weeks he hired the new man and gave him a route on Chicago's North Side and North Shore, from Irving Park Road, five miles from the heart of downtown, all the way to the far north suburb of Waukegan and from Lake Michigan to Western Avenue, three miles west.

One day on the elevator at Ontario Street, he met Jacob Cohn, who urged him to call on a West Side restaurant-owner (not in the territory just described) named Henry Arrighi. Mr. Arrighi used 150 pounds of coffee a week at his place at Van Buren and Paulina streets, but he wasn't using Continental. He once did, but a salesman had let him down, ignoring a problem Arrighi had with his coffee.

"Don't talk to me about Continental coffee," Mr. Arrighi told Mr. Pacini. "If you want to talk about something else, fine." They did talk about many other things. Their families had come from the same village in Italy, for one thing, and the two had much in common. For eight months the salesman visited the potential customer regularly. The two became friends but never talked about coffee that Mr. Arrighi might buy from Mr. Pacini.

They talked about coffee that others bought from Mr. Pacini, how Mr. Pacini's career was progressing, even about how Mr. Pacini went about convincing this or that prospect. It was a regular dance of the toreadors. Mr. Pacini would go through his routine with Mr. Arrighi, never suggesting he should buy his coffee, until one day — the charade at an end — Mr. Arrighi said he would do so. It was "one of the biggest thrills" of Mr. Pacini's career the day he sold Henry Arrighi, who had once said he would kick him out of his restaurant if he so much as mentioned Continental coffee.

The right contacts made all the difference in another early sale by Mr. Pacini, to Chicago's Mercy Hospital, where a buyer rebuffed him until he showed up with a note from his pastor. "I am sending Mr. Pacini, who has a very good coffee," the good father wrote. "Will you please talk to him?" The buyer did, and from the conversation came a 300-pound-a-week order. Walter Belinky, who knew all about the hard nut to crack at Mercy, was amazed.

But Mr. Pacini's top account in Chicago was the Lake Shore Athletic Club on Lake Shore Drive, a posh operation run by a Britisher named Nolan whom Mr. Pacini described decades later as "a lovely type of person." Six times Mr. Pacini called on the club, but the buyer was never available. The seventh time he went in not the front door but the rear of the building and made his way unannounced to Mr. Nolan's office. "I have a little package here. I would love to make some coffee for you," he told Mr. Nolan, and down to the kitchen they went. Mr. Pacini brewed some Continental coffee and gave Mr. Nolan the taste test, using numbered cups. The lovely Britisher picked Continental over the coffee the club was using, and Mr. Pacini had another big account.

The Georgian Hotel in north suburban Evanston was another big sale. For this one Mr. Pacini used an opposite tack. After several months of fruitless discussions with the hotel manager, he decided to go for the maitre d', a man named Victor. He told Victor one day that he had "something very interesting" to show him. It was a box with seven kinds of green coffee. He also had a "beautiful little grinder," which he used to grind some roasted-bean coffee on the spot for Victor. Victor tasted it and then picked up the beautiful little grinder and disappeared, leaving Mr. Pacini talking to the chef. In five minutes Victor returned without the grinder but with an order for 200 pounds of Mocha Java, Continental's top blend, to be delivered the following Thursday and weekly thereafter. The coffee salesman had scored again.

The coffee grinder was its own salesman. Mr. Pacini loaned a bigger, electric version out to substantial customers like the Georgian, who established it in full view and smelling distance of diners. These caught the aroma and knew how fresh the coffee was that they were drinking. At each table was placed a little card supplied by Mr. Pacini, saying: "We grind our coffee fresh just before you drink it. That's why it's so good." People loved it.

These five were the "field generals." All were on hand for the start of the second era of Continental history, its years of coffee expansion outside the Midwest in the '40s, '50s and '60s. They did more than any others to set the stage for that expansion, and they were part of it as well.

The 1930s was the time when that stage was set. The typical restaurant of the day was owner-operated, as opposed to today's chain operations, ranging from McDonald's to Holiday Inns. There were a few exceptions: Dario Toffenetti's five Chicago Loop restaurants and the Brass Rail eateries in New York City, for instance. But by and large, the restaurant of the 1930s was an owner-operated, modest affair where price mattered more than decor. To such individual owner-operators, service by a supplier on a personal basis was a highly valued commodity.

Into these restaurants in dozens of U. S. cities came the Continental Coffee Company route salesman, neatly even snappily dressed, to deliver coffee in 16-ounce white, blue or green bags — top-of-the-line "WB" blend or second-richest "Favorite" or the lighter-roast "76". Each bag held enough to make an urnful of coffee for those discriminating customers who came to eat and drink and who would leave the dining room remembering the coffee they drank at meal's end.

The salesman came weekly, delivering coffee roasted in most cases only a day or two earlier. He was careful to place the new bags in the rear of the restaurant's stock. With luck he would bring new coffee just as the previous week's supply was running out.

He checked the coffee-making equipment — the long thin gauge glass that ran down the outside of the urn, the urn bag into which dry coffee was placed before steaming hot water was poured over it, the urn itself. All of this was to make as sure as possible that the coffee delivered was brewed right. This combination sales and delivery man was also a roving critic of the quality of coffee as it was served.

The salesman collected payment from the restaurant operator if it was a cash account, got the invoice signed if a charge account. Having examined the customer's shelves, he told him what he needed and took next week's order on the spot. Then he returned to his half-ton panel truck waiting outside and headed for his next delivery. He made eighteen to twenty-five stops a day in this fashion.

Eighty to eighty-five percent of his sales were coffee. The rest were "allied" (food) products. A few salesmen, in Chicago and New York, drove one-ton trucks. Some preferred delivery sedans, or "sedan deliveries" as they were called, because they gave a sense of style to this hybrid, the salesman who was also a deliveryman. Kenny Babb in Champaign, Illinois, for instance, would reload his sedan, with its smaller capacity, in the middle of his twelve-hour working day, rather than drive a half-ton panel.

These were practitioners of what Jacob Cohn liked to call "belly to belly" selling on a weekly basis. There was no effort to get the Continental name up front, as in a grocery store. The salesman might offer Continental menu pads, but his product would not be advertised to the consumer in the usual sense. The product once sold to the restaurateur would be expected thereafter to sell itself.

To this end the salesman paid attention, as we have seen, not only to supplying the coffee but to brewing it as well.

Thus he provided urn bags and filter papers free of charge. The competition now did it, for one thing, and furthermore the company wanted its name kept in front of the restaurant owner. More important, such services were crucial to making sure the restaurant operators brewed and served coffee right and did not give in to the temptation to save a few dollars by using urn bags too often.

So route men sometimes changed bags, making sure they were clean. The coffee had to taste good. It was Jacob Cohn's contention that if diners were served good coffee, the last thing they had in a restaurant, they would come back. To the operators of finer restaurants, he would say: "You are serving good food. Serve good coffee as well."

The route salesman was at the heart of this process. The particulars of his work varied from city to city. In Chicago he might be only a 30-minute drive between his route and the Ontario Street headquarters. There he would arrive at day's end to sort things out at a small desk before dropping off his truck and going on home. Or if garage space was at a premium, he might take the truck with him and garage it himself overnight. On his way home, he might make a stop to drop off an item for a customer who had forgotten to order or who had run out — a gallon of salad dressing, for instance, or a carton of gelatin dessert.

In Pittsburgh, on the other hand, where his twenty or so stops a day were in both city and countryside, his travels took him far and wide. At the end of his day, furthermore, he would have to go to the truck terminal loading dock to load up for the next day's deliveries. This load he then took on home, where he kept it overnight and on weekends in his own garage at a $10 or so monthly charge to the company.

Pittsburgh and other salesmen outside Chicago arrived home between 6 P.M. and 8 P.M., later than Chicago salesmen, who did not have to load their own trucks. Shipping by truck became the norm during the 1940s, when train service became undependable. Over half the shipments from Chicago were by rail in 1940. But service slipped, and trucks became the preferred carrier for roasted coffee. Green coffee in porous burlap bags continued to be shipped by rail, though one load of this coffee arrived contaminated by a strong odor picked up in transit.

The truckers gave better service. Their problem was the increased danger of accident. Rarely did a railroad car roll off the track, but trucks sometimes rolled off roads, spilling or spoiling their cargo. Not often enough to rule out trucks, however.

For the good salesman in any market, Saturdays were for finding new business. He did this to a lesser extent during the week as well, in addition to his regular querying of customers: "No coffee? How about some salad dressing?" "We have a special on tea this week." "Try our new soup mix?"

Returns, as of gelatin or salad dressing, went back to the truck inventory. The less of this, the better, of course. The sheet for truck inventory was reviewed daily. If the driver carried too much, the office would complain. It was up to the driver, furthermore, to rotate his stock, putting his newest in the back of his truck. If he didn't, some coffee would be on trucks for weeks.

The whole process had to be monitored, of course. Thus an elaborate controls mechanism was devised to keep track of what left the plant and what was sold. To the outsider it was very complicated. It may best be described step by step.

INCOMING MAIL: In the day's mail were salesmen's orders for goods to be delivered the following week. These were clipped together. On top was an instruction sheet giving the date for the new batch of invoices, the date the goods were to leave the plant, their scheduled date of arrival and the trucking company that would deliver them. There were usually about twenty orders in each batch. Each order gave the customer's name and address, the blend of coffee he ordered in what size package, the total amount of coffee ordered and a list of allied products ordered. The orders went first to the order department, where they were billed.

BILLING: The order department did the billing with six-copy invoices. The first three went to shipping in a big envelope marked according to route, one per route. These were to be used by the salesman when he called on the customer to deliver and then take a new order. One was a customer copy, another was signed by the customer if it was a charge sale, and the third was used for writing down the new order. Being intended for the salesman, they were sent back to him with his merchandise in a carton marked with a big X so he could find them right off. The fourth copy also went to shipping, where it was used to fill orders. Also sent to shipping was the original order that had arrived in that day's mail, to be used as a check against the copies produced by the order department and the order filler. The fifth copy went to the matchup department, where it was used to make sure invoices sent to a salesman were returned. More on this later. The sixth copy was filed and kept for six to nine months.

CASHIER: Also in the mail from the salesman were the second copies of invoices for goods already delivered. Attached to these were checks from customers who had paid by check and a money order covering cash payments. The invoices for charge customers were signed by the customer. The cashier ran through these second copies to see if checks, money orders, and signed invoices balanced. Then she prepared checks and money orders for bank deposit. Then these second copies went to the matchup department.

MATCHUP: The matchup department checked these second copies to see that invoices sent to the salesmen were returned, without regard to whether payment was cash or charge. Not all were returned on time. Matchup would follow up on those that were not, notifying salesmen after five days. If this didn't work, the office manager would call the salesman.

INVENTORY: Matchup then sent the second copies to the salesman's inventory department, which recorded merchandise restored to the salesman's inventory and sold from it.

CREDIT: After invoices cleared the salesman's truck inventory department, they went to the credit department, where they were posted to accounts-receivable ledger cards. Cash accounts would show a debit and a credit and a zero balance, charge accounts only the debit. The ledger cards also showed how much coffee the customer bought each time. Thus if someone wanted to verify quickly a customer's coffee usage, the ledger cards were the way to find out.

SALES RUNUP: The second copies were finally sent to the sales runup department, where a young woman operating a comptometer, a tapeless adding machine, ran through the invoices route by route (in Chicago eighty or so routes) many times, totalling sales. One time was for coffee poundage by blend, another for units of allied products, another for the dollar value of each unit sold. The woman hung sheets containing these totals on a big peg board, one route after the other, so as to compile the total for each sales district. Equipment sales, that is, of Silex bowls and parts, filters, urns and urn parts, were listed in a column giving dollar amounts only. At the bottom of each column was a grand total of dollars per route per day. The whole procedure provided regular reports of coffee poundage and food products sales.

District sales managers were responsible for reviewing problem areas with their salesmen as regards customer deficiencies in payment. The credit department and the cashier worked closely in this area with the salesmen. When problems could not be resolved in this fashion, they contacted the sales manager.

The process continued in this fashion for decades. It was superseded only by the move to IBM data processing and the use of tab cards, followed eventually by computerized controls. But whatever the system, the big question has always been: how good are your controls? Any company, but especially one in a low-margin business, has to control the movement of merchandise or face inevitable serious problems of loss through oversight, theft or other kinds of shrinkage. Thus Continental's managers are constantly examining their controls for loopholes.

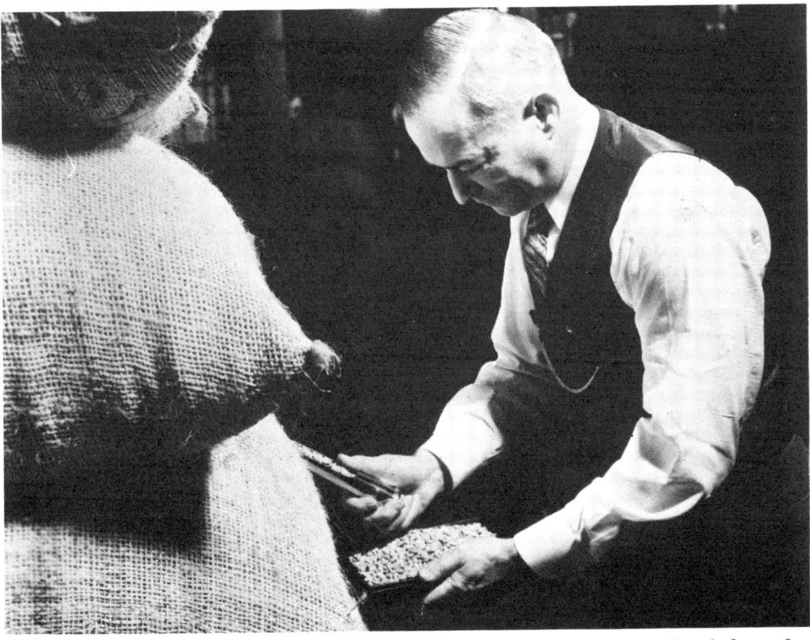

Coffee buyer Bill Meyer scoops coffee from a newly arrived bag for sample roasting. He uses a sharp-ended trowel-like tool to pierce the burlap and remove some coffee.

Green coffee arrives in 133-pound burlap bags in the mid-'40s at Ontario Street, where it is stored briefly on the fifth floor and then wheeled to the roasting machine.

3. GREEN COFFEE AND FOOD MANUFACTURING

During the 1930s patterns were set for Continental that never substantially changed. The buying of green coffee, for instance, was to remain essentially what it was for Jacob Cohn — a matter of buying and blending carefully, roasting and tasting a sample, making sure you had what you wanted.

The first thing a coffee company did was to buy green coffee beans. These came to the Ontario Street plant in 133-pound burlap bags from which samples were taken by plunging a sharp-ended scoop through the burlap and pulling out the coffee beans. Or a salesman might call with a sample. In either case the sample would be roasted on the fifth floor in a miniature roasting oven.

In the same room with the small tabletop roaster was a round table with a revolving stone top on which were slots for cups all around the edges. The sample roasted and ground, the grounds were placed in a cup. Then boiling water was poured over them, the mix was allowed to cool, and the taster spooned the liquid into his mouth. He kept it there long enough to get a taste, swishing it around, then spit it into a big brass spittoon off to one side on the floor.

Then with a slight movement of the table top, the taster put another cup in front of him, and so on, going all around the table if he wished. The coffee buyer was Bill Meyer, who began each day seated at the round table tasting coffee. Jacob

Green coffee samples are roasted in miniature roasters in the mid-'40s before tasting at the round stone table.

Coffee is roasted in quantity in the mid-'40s in the Thermalo roasters at the rate of more than 300 bags a day.

Cohn would join him there after he had seen all the trucks out and checked in at his office.

Each sat on a stool, bent over a coffee cup, spooning coffee out and into his mouth. Mr. Cohn had confidence in Mr. Meyer and backed him up if a green coffee salesman complained, as one did now and then, about his apparent rigidity in dealing with them when it came to the quality of their product.

Mr. Meyer was a one-man quality-control department and his word was law when it came to buying green coffee. He used to amaze some of his coworkers with his ability to have a nice lunch with several martinis and then return to coffee tasting with his ability unimpaired to tell good coffee from bad.

Once coffee arrived in the train yards, Mr. Meyer would order up carloads to a siding in the rear of the Ontario Street building. From each car was extended an aluminum chute down which were rolled the coffee-filled burlap bags to the first-floor level.

Day laborers did this unloading work beginning at 6:30 A.M. One would climb into the freight car, two others would wait on the floor below with skids. Each car carried 250 to 500 bags. When a skid was full, Sam Cohen, the elevator operator, would move it on a dolly to the elevator, then take it to the fifth-floor roasting area. After a certain number of elevator loads had been brought up, the unloaders would go to the fifth floor and there under Mr. Meyer's direction would unload the big bags, depositing them in piles according to how each was marked.

The Ontario Street building had little storage space; so coffee for the day's roasting had to be delivered each morning. Mr. Meyer would be stationed on the fifth floor all day long during the roasting, tasting samples of the roasted coffee. Consistent quality was the goal — not an easy matter because not all the coffee had matured at the same time. It was an art (later to be made something of a science as well) to make sure coffee tasted right.

Coffee was bought primarily through salesmen who brought samples. If the salesman's sample passed the taste test, coffee was bought subject to further sampling on delivery. If sampling of delivered coffee led to its approval, it was roasted in full quantities, tested all along the way, as we have seen.

The sellers were brokers who dealt directly with planters, many of them in Brazil. Mr. Cohn made at least one Brazil trip with his family in the early '30s, mainly as vacation. While there, he bought coffee; but this was the exception.

The coffee would be bought on a 90-day letter of credit. An "ocean bill of lading" was given as receipt of shipment. This was good for money at the bank to the shipper. On payment to the shipper, the bank activated the letter of credit (made the loan), with the amount due in ninety days at a low 3/8 of 1% interest paid by Continental.

In ninety days the coffee would be roasted and sold, and the company could then pay off the letter of credit. This is how the company financed its coffee buying for years.

Once in the '50s, Jacob Cohn deviated from this "ocean bill of lading" procedure, which stated that the coffee was on shipboard. Instead, he made a sizable purchase of Brazilian coffee at a good price direct from the Brazilian company (not from a broker) and got in return a warehouse receipt.

He had dealt with this company and knew of its good reputation; so he saw little risk of the purchase not working out. What he didn't know was that the company had new owners.

The coffee mysteriously disappeared from the warehouse, and Continental was stuck with a loss of between $250,000 and $500,000. It was a sign of the company's strength that it was able to sustain such a loss. Not long after that, in 1954, the company opened its green coffee buying office in New York with John Heuman in charge.

Another venture in buying direct from the source and not

from a broker was the purchase by Continental, also in the '50s, of half interest in Rehteleu Coffee Company in Guatemala. Continental bought green coffee through this company for about five years. Another Guatemalan venture was the purchase of a coffee mill, where Continental dried and processed Guatemalan coffee.

Aside from some episodes such as these, coffee buying was not much different in the mid-1960s, when Continental reached its peak of coffee sales, from in the 1930s. Samples were still roasted in miniature ovens, then ground, then given the taste test by experts sitting at a revolving round table.

An expert coffee taster could check fifteen cups in thirty seconds, a brochure says. The green coffee division, opened in 1954 on New York's Front Street, the center of U. S. coffee marketing, had its own membership on the New York Coffee and Sugar Exchange. The green coffee department moved to Chicago in 1972.

On the other hand, roasting was quite a bit more mechanized. Procedures once done by hand, laboriously on the hottest and coldest of days, were now done by machine in plants from coast to coast. Green coffees were fed first into a cleaner and then in 3,000-pound batches into a blending drum to assure consistency.

Then the blended coffee was roasted, cooled and ground in grinders that could grind 2,500 pounds an hour. After grinding, the coffee was packaged by machines that weighed, filled and sealed 10,000 packages a day. Roasted samples were cup-tested along the way.

In fact, coffee was cup-tested four times in all: in samples before it was ordered, when it arrived at dockside in a freighter, when it arrived at the roasting plant, and then during the roasting process.

By now also, the art of making coffee had become more scientific. In the Continental laboratory, coffee was sifted through four screens of varying meshes. The amount of coffee

By the 1960s roasters were equipped with electronically controlled thermostats and timers, but it was still the operator's "trained eye and nose" that judged aroma and color.

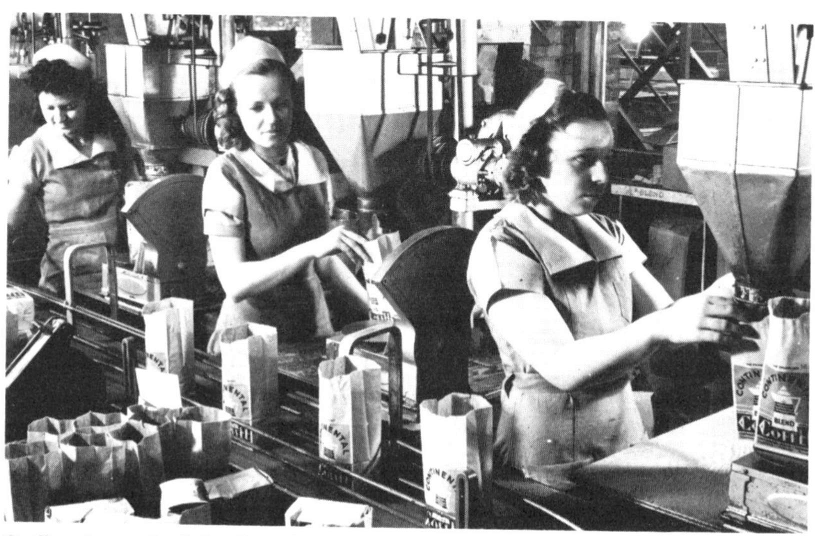

Coffee is packed by hand in Chicago. Each packer packs a different blend, holding the bags under the chutes which are fed by overhead pipes.

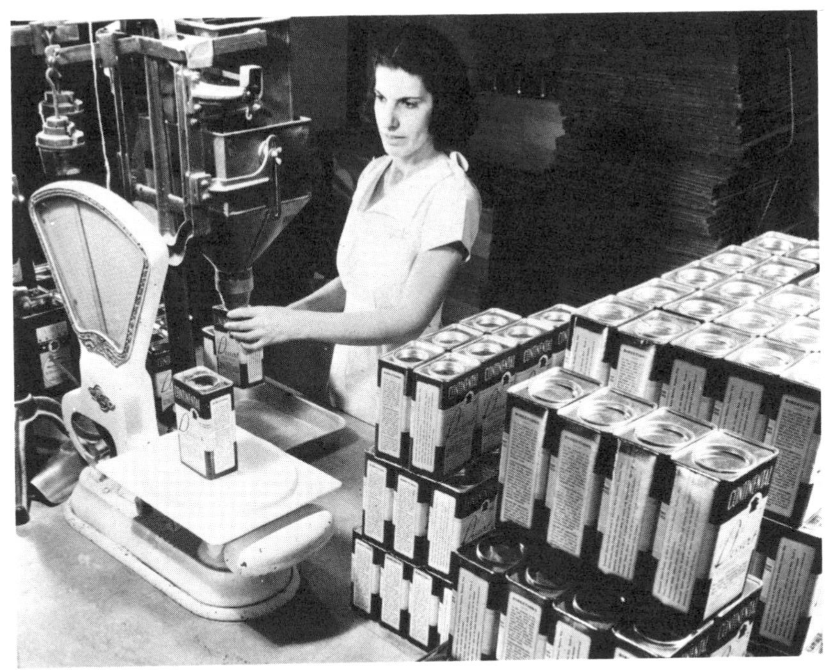

Gelatin and cream desserts, among the earliest of "allied" products, are packed at Ontario Street.

deposited on each screen was measured to tell whether the ground coffee conformed to the grind specification. Color analysis measured flavor development.

The roasters had electronically controlled thermostats and timers, but it was still the operator's "trained eye and nose" that judged aroma and color, according to a 1965 brochure.

Five years later, in April, 1970, the coffee was blended by computer, and an automatic packaging line could turn out 25,000 packages a day.

Coffee in the 1930s was the heart of Continental's business. But the early '30s marked the start of another part of that business, the manufacture or processing of non-coffee food products. In 1933 Jacob Cohn hired a man named John Gamma, who began to make steak sauce, chocolate syrup, fudge sauce and the like for selling to restaurants along with the coffee. Tea and spices were part of the original product mix also.

Continental realized that customers found it more convenient and efficient to use "a few dependable suppliers, rather than many," and so it made sense to multiply the line of products, according to a 1970 brochure. This may have been to attribute some mid-'60s thinking to Jacob Cohn in the early '30s. In any event, it was decided to set up "one of the first research labs devoted to the needs of the away-from-home food service industry."

Out of this lab came the first of Continental's so-called "allied" products, including desserts and salad dressings. The time apparently had come for this idea, because by the end of the decade the foods division, as it became known, quadrupled in size from its beginning years.

Steve Galvin came in 1937 to head the operation. There were two others as well, one a food chemist and the other a packaging and marketing specialist, who made foodservice history in 1939. The chemist was George Sternfield and the packaging and marketing man was Bob Rosenthal. The chemist created a dehydrated soup mix, one of the first food mixes to which hot water was added to prepare the product or, seen another way, one of the first "fast foods."

This is the history part, but not all. The product succeeded within a year or so, in both retail and institutional markets — though in the latter there was resistance from chefs, who as a rule preferred their soup to anyone else's, including a highly suspect substance to which you simply added hot water.

The new dry soup was marketed by a newly established subsidiary, Continental Foods, which sold to Continental Coffee Company in the institutional market and to other distributors in the retail market.

The future for the new product was bright, except that Continental Coffee Company could not afford to finance its rapid expansion. Meanwhile, the giant Lipton Tea Company, looking about for just such a product, discovered Continental Foods and after an extended negotiation bought it in the summer of 1941.

Mr. Cohn agreed to the sale (at a good price) in part to give Messrs. Rosenthal and Sternfield a chance to benefit from association with a company big enough to develop their product at a rapid rate.

Continental Coffee Company continued to market the soup — produced by Lipton in Hoboken, New Jersey — to institutional customers under its own label. When Lipton a few years later found itself unable to fill Continental's orders, Continental was allowed to make the product, which it continued to distribute under the Continental label.

Another reason for selling Continental Foods was that as a retail operation it constituted an unaccustomed cash drain. Retail sales involved payment delays that did not sit well with the essentially wholesale function of the coffee company.

By the 1940s, Continental was selling food at the rate of $75,000 a month — a far cry from the $100 a week assigned as a goal to driver-salesman Joe Davis when the first of these products came out.

In 1940, Jack Bloom joined the company as assistant to Steve Galvin, who headed food manufacturing. Mr. Bloom, Jacob Cohn's nephew, was from Centerville, Iowa, the home town of many a Continental employee of those days, as we have seen.

When Mr. Galvin left Continental Coffee Company for Lipton with the dry-soup operation a year later, Mr. Bloom took over food manufacturing. He already had an undergraduate degree in chemistry from the University of Chicago. Late in 1942 he began a doctoral program at his alma mater which led to his receiving a doctorate in organic chemistry in December of 1945.

Jack Bloom became the guiding light for Continental's food

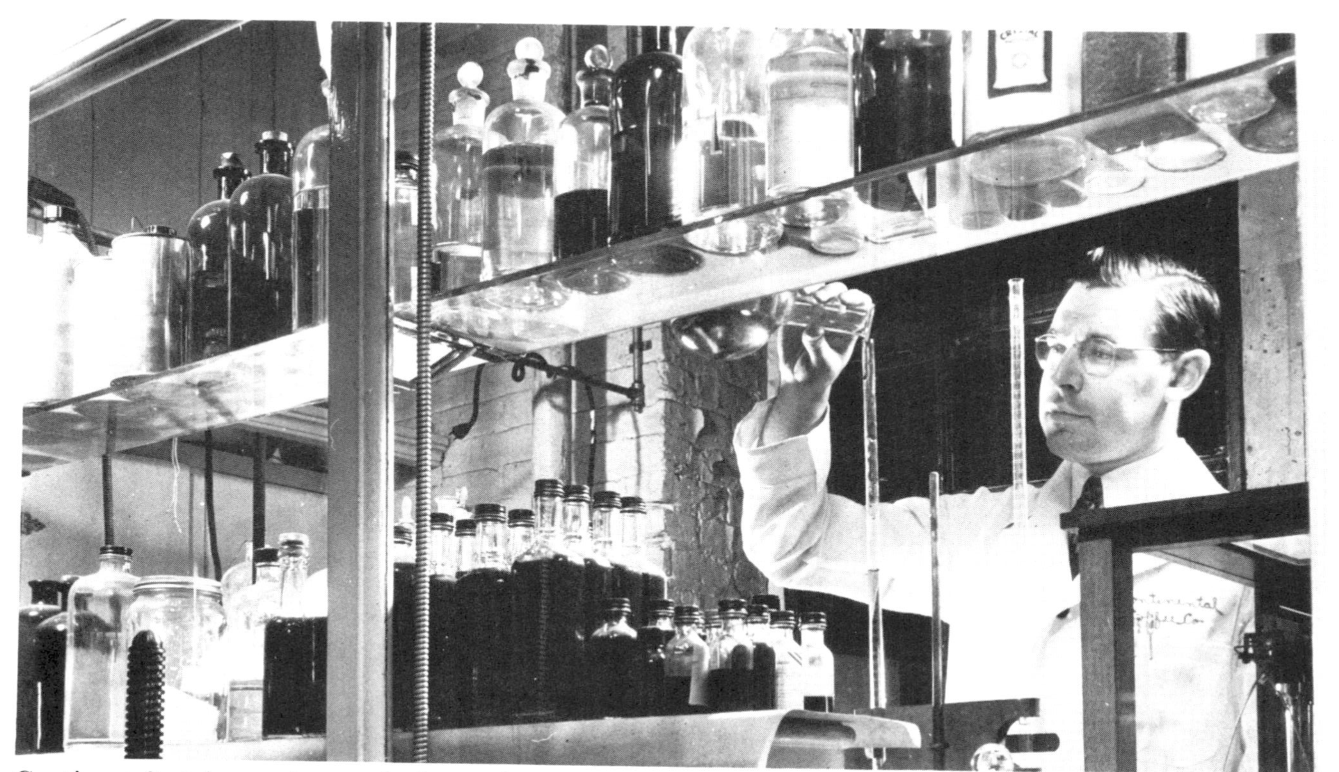

Continental's laboratories sought by testing to improve products and develop new ones. Here a chemist is at work at Ontario Street in the '50s.

processing department and its laboratory effort to his retirement in October of 1984. He earned the doctorate while working thirty hours a week for Continental and about the same amount for the U. S. Navy on a project based at the University of Chicago campus. All that plus his school work added up to a ninety-hour week, enough to keep a young man busy.

At Continental he headed the food operation. It was World War II, and materials were rationed. Vegetable oil was in short supply; so Continental reduced its production of mayonnaise, which was 80% oil, in favor of salad dressing, which was 25%. Another change was to oil-free French dressing to which customers could add oil if they chose.

Glass jars were scarce; so salesmen were instructed to retrieve them from customers when they had used up their contents. Returned to the Ontario Street plant, the jars were re-used after being washed in a washing machine bought specially for the purpose. Continental also saved on metal by using a narrow-necked jar which required smaller caps. In working out these and other solutions, Jack Bloom was a committee of one, beating to the punch big companies like General Foods, where channels seemed to slow the decision process.

Laboratory research continued into the '50s and '60s. Private-label barbecue and steak sauces were made for restaurant chains — Ponderosa and McDonald's among them — to their specifications. In Chicago, Wimpy's hamburger chain was a customer. For a hotel chain in the Northwest U. S., Continental made green goddess and caesar dressings. Specialty dressing sales showed gains of up to seventy-five percent a year during the mid-60s.

A new cole-slaw dressing test-marketed positive. The testing process was part of the food-manufacturing way of doing things. Some decades earlier, in the mid-'40s, there had been a question of using rich European chocolate, with its tart, even bitter flavor, or sweeter milk chocolate. Continental's testing had shown that drinkers of hot chocolate generally favored milkier, sweet chocolate over the darker European chocolate which its supplier, Nestlé, produced. So Continental dropped Nestlé chocolate and began making its own.

In the '70s sweetness fell into disrepute, however, and Continental produced newly popular diet products such as low-calorie and low-salt dressings and soups.

Over the decades there was work also with detergents and cleaning compounds, including development of three or four dishwashing compounds. It was part of Continental's ability to meet almost every need of the restaurant operator, in the kitchen as well as in the dining room.

Lab research up to the early '60s was in coffee production more than anything else, however, much of it connected with the vending industry. Coffee research apart from vending is what made of coffee blending and roasting something more than the judgment of the man on the spot.

What made a science of coffee blending was linear programming, a computer-directed system that quantifies the blending process. The blender decides on five ingredients of a good blend, and the program provides their lowest-cost combination. It's a way of numerically defining the components of good coffee to "maximize flavor," as Dr. Bloom explains it.

Continental coffee researchers also developed nitrogen-packing of coffee in laminated plastic bags. Vacuum-packed cans, standard for retail use, were inconvenient and expensive for the institutional market. So Continental developed a process of replacing the air in coffee bags with nitrogen. Coffee packed this way stayed fresh for two or three months, giving the product a much extended shelf life and incidentally eliminating the need for the weekly salesman's visit, at least to smaller customers. The labs also encouraged use of paper-filter coffee bags with pre-measured amounts of coffee for use in vending machines. These bags were discarded after use, with the grounds still inside.

Furthermore, the brewing equipment itself was simplified,

so that by the '70s a waitress had only to press a button on a self-contained counter-top brewer to make coffee. This eliminated the guesswork and removed much of the drudgery from the job, which once called for pouring just the right amount of water into the top of an urn.

The lab also explored use of charcoal water filters in areas with water problems and found they protected coffee taste much better than water-softeners. Charcoal filters eliminated the "off odors" from minerals that give coffee an odd taste, not to mention food products that use water. The company also pioneered the use of free-flowing blends for fresh-brew coffee-vending machines, of which more later.

Among later food developments was the introduction in the '70s of Jellite, a gelatin-like dessert packed ready to eat in a plastic cup and requiring no refrigeration. It was "ideally suited" to a proposed federal school lunch program, according to a 1970 brochure. The same brochure tells of a "dust-free all-purpose cocoa mix" for vending machines and canned chicken, ham and tuna-salad sandwich spread for fast-food operators and food service companies.

Continental technologists were performing more than three dozen kinds of tests on Continental products in the late '60s. Ingredients were checked daily for a total of 20,000 tests in all during 1969. Some tests were of food products, answering questions like: "How thick is the salad dressing? How much oil in the mayonnaise? How much moisture in the cocoa? How well does the gelatin set? What is the consistency of the portion-packed jelly?"

Packaging was its own story. Coffee was sold in more than 200 kinds and sizes. Kits for office coffee services, for instance, accounted for 150 million cups a year. Food was packed in sizes ranging from tiny portion packs of jelly, mustard and ketchup to five-gallon drums.

A diner's favorite meal away from home might have begun with Continental soup — ham, onion, beef or chicken. Continental "roast saver" might have added flavor to the meat and made gravy for mashed potatoes. The condiments might have included individual servings of Continental ketchup and mustard and one or more of Continental's table sauces — barbecue, Worcestershire, steak and chop, chop suey. Dessert might have been one of seven Continental gelatins or one of five cream puddings or pie fillings.

Whatever the combination, the Continental-fed diner was reaping the benefits of what was started in the early '30s when Continental's food-manufacturing operation was begun.

PART TWO

Coffee to the Nation

4. WORLD WAR II

In 1940, when Stanley Owens began at Continental, the company fully deserved the name Continental Coffee Company. Coffee was 90% of its business, the rest being so-called "allied products" — salad dressings and other non-coffee restaurant staples.

Mr. Owens had been with Mesirow & Co., a securities firm, for five years, after earning an accounting degree from Northwestern University in 1934. As a younger man growing up in Chicago's Hyde Park neighborhood, he had played baseball and basketball for Hyde Park High School and done impressions in Chicago theaters and night clubs of Amos 'n' Andy and others, appearing in shows featuring top performers. He had entered Northwestern in 1930, having decided by then against the stage performer's life and in favor of the businessman's. Beginning in 1935 at Mesirow, he liked the work, but he also got a 1930s view of the securities business as a fairly risky enterprise.

At the same time, he got a look at one of Mesirow's clients, for whom the firm hedged coffee futures and handled personal investments — a short, stocky man in his 40s who sold coffee to restaurants. This man was Jacob Cohn.

Mr. Owens was impressed with how Mr. Cohn handled himself, and the coffee business looked good to him too. He knew Continental had done well during the past ten years, which

The young Art Ames sits (*second from left*) at a table in the Continental Coffee exhibit at the annual restaurant convention at Chicago's Stevens (now Conrad Hilton) Hotel, 1940.

had been terribly unkind at times to securities. He told Mr. Cohn he'd like to work for him. To Mr. Cohn he seemed to be an eager, competent young man with an eye for opportunity, his kind of man, with a leg up on the financial aspects of business to boot. He had a flickering recollection of his own problems. Young Owens might be someone who could help him out of some current difficulties in his own operation.

Mr. Cohn told Mr. Owens he could use him but that Mr. Owens should first talk to his boss Norman Mesirow and tell him that Mr. Owens's leaving was his idea and not Mr. Cohn's. Jacob Cohn was not about to pirate help from his broker, and he didn't want to look like he was doing it either. Mr. Owens went to Mr. Mesirow and paved the way for his friendly departure.

Mr. Owens arrived at Continental Coffee headquarters at 371-375 West Ontario Street, on Chicago's Near North Side to find a successful family operation whose sixty driver-salesmen were moving five million pounds of coffee a year.

Art Ames, a recent graduate of the University of Illinois at the tender age of nineteen, was already there. Mr. Ames had joined the company just as war broke out in Europe, in September, 1939, hiring on at $17 a week as factotum assistant ("go-fer") to the sales manager, the redoubtable Walter Belinky. He worked briefly for Mr. Belinky before Mr. Belinky left the firm, to return some years later, after the war. Mr. Ames left the firm in April, 1942, when he entered the Army.

The young Ames, later an executive with a major competitor on the West Coast, could have done worse than be exposed to such as Mr. Belinky, who is credited by many as having contributed much to building the Continental sales operation through his innovative sales-management techniques and his ability to inspire and/or intimidate the sales force so that it mounted superior efforts.

The company had been growing for more than two decades. Its sales force had expanded in a manner unheard of for a route business in an age before freeways, when two-lane highways and railroads were the only way to move the goods from city to city.

Moving the merchandise was a major challenge. Coffee had to be at restaurants hundreds of miles away within two or three days after it was roasted in Chicago or New York. It was packed in bags lined with glassine, a thin but tough near-transparent paper used also as windows for envelopes. Its freshness was therefore a delicate thing.

More than coffee was being sold, of course. Tea, spices and powdered hot chocolate had been staples for the company almost from its inception. From the early '30s the so-called "allied products" line of foodstuffs had also been sold and delivered from those half-ton brown and green panel trucks with bold chromium lettering along the sides. These allied products, as we have seen, ranged from salad dressings, near the beginning of a meal, to gelatin desserts at its end.

Walter Belinky was at the heart of the sales process. Praised by many as a writer of brochures, letters, booklets and the like, he was at the height of his form as an inspirer, organizer and even conscience for Continental salesmen. To a man in the field he would dictate a letter that would lift him from the dumps. His trips to the field would make salesmen do just a little better job than usual and might perk the man up in the process. He had a fantastic ability to remember names, and his sales meeting performances were superb. He led a hard life for Continental, on the road forty weeks out of the year, but as a bachelor without family he didn't seem to mind it. His business was his hobby, he said later.

Mr. Belinky was not alone in his dedication to the work at hand. "An unbelievable feeling of loyalty" permeated Continental recalls Art Ames. "If the leader [Jacob Cohn] said employees should work for nothing for a year, they would have said, 'So what?' You would go to the moon for him, and he would never forget you."

Successful sales management techniques were taken for granted. The "sandwich method" of correcting a salesman was standard practice, for instance: sandwich a reprimand between two compliments, even if the supervisor had to dig deep for the compliments.

Hiring and training salesmen was reduced to a system: new hires almost always started in the shipping room, for instance, so that when they hit the road they knew order-filling inside and out. And not only salesmen. Administrative personnel took turns, if brief, in the shipping room and on sales routes.

Still it was wartime, with the inconveniences and even hardships that entailed. By the early '40s, there was rationing of sugar and vegetable oil, which had its impact on the food-service industry. Continental was able to adapt more quickly than bigger operations, developing a sugarless gelatin dessert six months after rationing began, for instance — the first in the institutional field to do so.

Wartime adaptation took another form when it came to pasta, which as the war years unfolded became an entree of choice for meat-starved restaurateurs. Pasta — whether noodles, spaghetti or some other configuration of this infinitely malleable product — began to develop premium status.

Continental's supplier began to see sales possibilities that went beyond what he could achieve in serving his old customers, whose purchases were to be at frozen prices. His new customers, on the other hand, were permitted to pay more than the government-determined price, and Continental began to find its orders shorted.

Enter the Dziurgots. Jacob Cohn put it to Stan Owens that Continental Coffee Company might buy a pasta maker. Mr. Owens advertised for a seller but got no response; so, ever the direct problem-solver, he looked up pasta-makers in the telephone book and began calling them.

Not the big guys, like Red Cross, but ones who might like the idea of being bought by a coffee company. He called John

Dziurgot & Sons, got one of the sons, and told him what he wanted. The son got back to him in a few days and said, "Let's talk." His father, who spoke only Polish but understood English, would be there. The two sons would do the talking.

The father was interested, and the sons were delighted when they were told the deal would require their staying on to run the place. Mr. Owens brought Jacob Cohn to meet the Dziurgots — the brothers and their seventy-year-old father, ailing and thus willing to sell.

It was an only-in-America scene: immigrant dealing with immigrant. The old man speaking no English meeting the younger man who had learned it as a boy of eight or nine. The Pole who made pasta, an Italian specialty, and the Central European Jew who once sold coffee from a horse-drawn wagon and now from a fleet of trucks. The two of them cementing a business agreement in Chicago while the homelands each had left decades earlier suffered grievously in the midst of an atrocious war.

Mr. Cohn was impressed with the brothers, hard-working men about his age, who when told Continental would be using their entire capacity said that would be fine with them: they would simply work even harder and keep up with their current customers as well.

With the Dziurgot pasta came the Dziurgot building, in the 1800 block of West North Avenue. Continental sold this building a few years later, in 1946, when it acquired a triangular structure at Milwaukee Avenue and Hubbard Street which had housed the McKenney Importing Company, a coffee importer. Continental bought the McKenney business and integrated it into its own.

It was not clear at first, however, that the pasta plant, now the Grand Olivier Food Company, could be moved at all. Its 15-foot wooden rooms for drying the pasta presented a challenge even to the hardworking Dziurgots and their helper, Tom Frontera.

They did it, however. Working overtime, the Dziurgots and Mr. Frontera moved the driers to the Milwaukee-and-Hubbard building without missing a minute of production time. The years had caught up with the Dziurgots, however, and the two brothers announced their retirement.

Tom Frontera would run the operation for Continental in their place. "We Poles aren't the real pasta-makers," one of the brothers told Stan Owens. "Tom Frontera [who was of Italian ancestry] can run it for you. He works as hard as we do." From then on, Mr. Frontera was in charge.

This didn't mean the Dziurgots weren't available, however. One of the brothers called weekly for a month thereafter, asking Mr. Owens if Continental needed any help, which he offered free of charge.

Pasta-making changed, however. Always highly competitive, it became even more so as the old wooden "dry rooms" became obsolete. Continental, never a big producer and not about to invest in the new equipment, liquidated Grand Olivier and sold the building in 1962. Tom Frontera who had run the operation with the help of his wife Rose, continued in Continental's employ, retiring as a plant security guard in 1969. His two daughters worked at the time for Continental. The building at Milwaukee and Hubbard in 1985 housed a construction firm, its pasta-making days gone forever.

Wartime adaptation took many forms, including hiring an under-age but able-bodied high-school dropout named Joe Harjung to work as a coffee packager for seventy-five cents an hour. A strapping 15-year-old, Mr. Harjung was hired without a work permit by the plant foreman at Ontario Street, Harry Rafal, who assumed the lad was at least sixteen.

Once Mr. Rafal realized he had robbed the classroom if not the cradle for his new recruit, he sent young Harjung downtown for the permit. But the kid returned without it, pleading he'd been too embarrassed to admit he was so young. Mr. Rafal let it slide for the months remaining before the boy came of working age, and thus began Mr. Harjung's career with Continental, which in time took him to California as a plant supervisor.

More Huck Finn than Horatio Alger, he knew more about the streets of Chicago's Old Town neighborhood when he was hired than he did about production schedules or even basic business practices. But three weeks after he started at Ontario Street, he was in the stock room, filling orders for ten cents more an hour than when he started.

Mr. Harjung returned to school after a time, finishing at Chicago's Lane Tech, a boys' college-prep public school. Even there, he was as good at hooky as anything else, using an early-dismissal pass of his own devising to get himself and his cronies out early to catch a movie downtown or a Cubs game.

At Continental Jacob Cohn gave him a copy of the Dale Carnegie book, *How to Win Friends and Influence People,* and later Mr. Harjung took university courses in management at company expense. He never did get a college degree, however. He says he would not be hired now for the work he does for Continental, managing fast-food shortening production on the West Coast.

He shakes his head sometimes as he considers the unwillingness of many employees today to identify with the company. "When I did something, I was Continental," he says. His pride was wrapped up in it. It was (and remains) something he felt responsible for.

For Joe Harjung and others, the Ontario Street plant and company headquarters apparently was a sort of home away from home. People felt comfortable there. Even an outsider could sense it. One of these was Jerome S. Gore, now chairman emeritus of Hartmarx Corporation and presiding co-chairman of the Chicago and Northern Illinois region of the National Conference of Christians and Jews.

As a young man just out of college in the early '40s, Mr. Gore helped Leichinger, Bennett & Co. audit the firm's books.

He recalls what a pleasant place it was. One of the things he remembers was the coffee, tea and hot chocolate which a young woman brought around to people in the office.

This was 20-year-old Stella Craglione. Her role was to supply for employees a short break in their work day. It was a coffee break, obviously. Mr. Cohn had seen something like it in New Orleans in 1939 and had adopted the practice for Continental, which became one of the first American businesses to do it.

"Coffee, tea or hot chocolate?" Miss Craglione asked at each desk, once in mid-morning and again in mid-afternoon, offering cream or sugar to go with it, free of charge. Neat, smiling, friendly in her white uniform, she served from a cart fitted with Bunsen burners which kept the coffee and hot water warm.

The aisle she went to first on Monday was second on Tuesday, and so forth. There was a system to it. It was an institution, an amenity that helped set the tone for the place, Jacob Cohn's solution to the problem how employees might find a few minutes respite without leaving their desks.

Royal F. Munger, of the *Chicago Daily News,* described its effect: "At 3:30 work stopped and waitresses wheeled in carts with crackers and cups of steaming tea and coffee. A warm drink, a few moments to stop and chat, and life began to look brighter. Even salesmen waiting in the reception room . . . usually the most bored and sad of mortals, cheered up and began to smile at each other."

What was good for Continental would be good for other companies, management decided. After three years of experiencing the benefits of its own coffee break, the company sent out a letter to other companies offering to help "institute a similar program" with "very little expense."

Besides Continental's free coffee break, its employees could buy coffee, tea and other Continental products at a 20 percent discount. Mr. Cohn in fact wanted them to drink Continental

THE CHICAGO DAILY NEWS

THURSDAY, OCTOBER 24, 1940.

"Old Bill" Suggests—

At the offices of the Continental Coffee Company, in Chicago, the long afternoon was dragging wearily toward 3:30 p. m. Not that there wasn't plenty of work to be done. Six carloads of coffee were on the spur track for unloading, the shipping department was piled up with orders, the roasters were going at capacity, and the department which manufactures coffee urns was so piled up with orders that the foreman was considering an extra shift. The company employs about 250 people, and is the largest coffee importer and roaster distributing to hotels and restaurants. But in any business, when the first freshness of the day has worn off, and it is still a long way to quitting time, there is a certain letdown.

Then, at 3:30, work stopped in the offices and waitresses wheeled in tea carts with crackers and cups of steaming tea and coffee. A warm drink, a few moments to stop and chat, and life began to look brighter. Even the salesmen waiting in the reception room for a chance to see the head of the company, who usually are the most bored and sad of mortals, cheered up and began to smile at each other. As an inquiring reporter, merely watching the process of coffee roasting, we happened to arrive in time for a cup, and felt much the better.

It seems that a year ago the president of the company was visiting New Orleans (much of the coffee that goes into his blends comes by ship from South America and thence by rail to Chicago) and saw a similar practice there. He introduced it in his company, and now the organization couldn't get along without it. The idea struck us as worth mentioning, partly because it tends to reintroduce into business some of the small amenities lost in the search for the hard fetish of efficiency. Perhaps there is no efficiency lost, for as we left, a waitress was col-

An account of the Continental coffee break that appeared in the *Chicago Daily News.*

Ontario Street office staff in August of 1942.

coffee. He wanted them to enjoy and be proud of their product.

All was not coffee breaks, of course. These were crucial years for the company. Walter Belinky left, to return several years later. Leon and Joseph Katz also went elsewhere, leaving important managerial gaps.

Jacob Cohn's sons Alvin and Robert, later to take the reins of leadership, were not yet of an age to do so. Alvin did join the company about midway through this period, having earlier worked routes during college summers; but by mid-1942 he was off to military service.

Leon Katz was treasurer, general manager and second in command. His brother Joe was in charge of Chicago city sales. Their sister Toby was receptionist and switchboard operator. Among them, they controlled access to Jacob Cohn.

If this was a problem, as some believe it was, the hiring of Stan Owens was its solution, because in Mr. Owens, an accountant and financial man with an eagle's eye for detail and unquestioned loyalty, he found someone to take Leon Katz's place, a first assistant who over the years was not only to help shepherd the company through many changes but was to become practically a member of the family.

In six months he was controller, having worked for part of that time with Leon, who left Continental in the fall of 1941. Mr. Owens became general manager. He was to be Jacob Cohn's right-hand man over the next twenty-eight years, providing an essential gluing and lubricating function for the rapidly growing and changing firm. It was a very important changing of the guard, comparable to the rise to leadership of Jacob Cohn's sons a decade later.

The Continental sales force for Michigan and Ohio met at Chicago's Stevens Hotel in November of 1940. Jacob Cohn is at far end. Second from his left is coffee buyer Bill Meyer. To the far right, standing, is Stanley Owens. Seated nearest the camera, in the center, is Simon Rice, later Brooklyn branch manager.

5. NEW YORK

The world's fair in New York City in 1939 led to Continental's first coffee roasting outside Chicago. Dario Toffenetti, owner of five Toffenetti restaurants in Chicago, announced that he had secured a restaurant concession. Mr. Toffenetti was going to the fair, and Continental decided to follow him.

Coffee roasted in Chicago could not be shipped to New York with its required Continental freshness. If the company let Mr. Toffenetti go without them, Mr. Toffenetti, a major customer, might turn to others for his coffee needs. Besides, the world's fair was bound to generate a great deal of business. In this respect it would give Continental an opportunity to enter a new market with adequate startup volume. Mr. Toffenetti later opened a very large restaurant on Times Square after the fair.

As to possibly losing even the Chicago Toffenetti business, Mr. Toffenetti had already said that if a competitor's coffee brewed better, that coffee would be his choice. Indeed, Mr. Toffenetti periodically called in other companies to compare their products, and if he found a better-tasting coffee, Continental would lose his account.

Mr. Cohn had himself won Mr. Toffenetti's business only after visiting his place repeatedly until the day came when Mr. Toffenetti had complaints from customers. At that point he called Mr. Cohn and asked him to bring in some Continen-

Jacob Cohn and his chief aides, Chicago, August of 1942, *clockwise beginning at front left:* Alvin Cohn, Stanley Owens, Dick McAllister, Bill Meyer, Aaron A. Good.

tal coffee, in order to taste it. Persistence had won out. This is why Mr. Cohn regularly visited customers' restaurants, to stay in touch with them and to make sure the coffee was tasting good.

Once Mr. Toffenetti did have a problem and put in a call on a Saturday morning to Stanley Owens at his Ontario Street office. "The coffee's tasting bad," he said. "I want you to come over and taste it." Mr. Owens promised to come right over.

Mr. Owens doubted his own coffee-tasting abilities, however, and put in a call to the company's coffee-buyer and chief taster, Bill Meyer, at his Wilmette home. "Can you meet me at Toffenetti's on Randolph Street?" Mr. Owens asked him. Mr. Meyer, who was cutting his grass at the time, said he'd be there.

The two met and went inside. Mr. Meyer tasted the coffee black. There was nothing wrong with it. He asked the waitress to pour in cream. She did, and parts of it laid there atop the coffee.

Toffenetti came out of the kitchen and was told his cream was curdled. Expressionless, he thanked the two Continental troubleshooters and returned immediately to the kitchen, most likely to find out why his people were serving bad cream with good coffee.

In Brooklyn, Continental set up a roasting plant at 199 Steuben Street, later moving to a long, narrow, three-story building at 471 Hudson Avenue, a half block from the Paramount Theatre in the middle of Brooklyn's business section. Yet later it was moved to larger quarters on Long Island.

In the Steuben Street building were two roasters, two lines for odd-size coffee packages, and a machine that bagged and sealed the standard 16-ounce packages. The Toffenetti world's fair and restaurant accounts were big and profitable, but in 1939 and the early '40s, the Brooklyn operation was a loser.

"We lost a lot of money in New York," recalls Alvin Cohn, Jacob's eldest son. Enough, in fact, to make the father consider selling the New York operation. He even had a meeting with Old Dutch Coffee Company about a possible sale. Alvin, on the verge of leaving school to get married, urged him not to sell.

On Nov. 20, 1941, Alvin Cohn did get married and after honeymooning in Florida took the train straight to New York to take over the operation there. Meeting him and his wife Lorraine at the train station was Stanley Owens, who had suggested the move to Jacob Cohn.

"Alvin should have a chance to work on his own," Mr. Owens had told Jacob Cohn, who decided the idea was a good one but only if Mr. Owens helped his son, not yet twenty-one years old, get settled in the big, strange city.

They stayed at the St. George Hotel, the biggest in Brooklyn, and not at the Park Central, in Manhattan, where Mr. Owens had booked rooms, because Alvin Cohn was intent on making the St. George a Continental customer.

The day after Alvin arrived to head the Brooklyn branch,

Aaron A. Good and Stanley Owens, August of 1942.

Alvin Cohn, August of 1942.

three women employees quit. Alvin asked the third why the exodus, and she candidly explained, "We have nothing to do and knew you'd find out, so we left." Later two of the five route salesmen quit or were let go for the same reason: there were too many people doing not enough work. There were reasons why Brooklyn was floundering.

Alvin went selling and learned a thing or two, some of it heartening, some discouraging. He was stunned when a customer asked him how many "cars" (boxcars) he had of tomato juice. Alvin was used to selling by the can or at most the case. He was not so stunned that he didn't move to make the sale, calling his father in Chicago for a price on the huge quantity.

Alvin came through with the tomato juice, and the big customer asked if he had any more. The first order of two cars was a $7,000 sale. The young man from Chicago managed to sell seven cars.

On the other hand, he was hamstrung in the midst of another big sale when coffee rationing was imposed and coffee companies found themselves limited to three-fourths of their previous year's coffee sales. He landed two big New York-based accounts — Liggett's Drugs and the Union News Company, which regardless of its name was an operator of restaurants in train stations coast to coast — but had to give them up when it became clear that Continental couldn't service them without shorting established customers. The decision was a stunningly ethical one. Many's the company which would not have hesitated to do whatever it took to gain the new accounts, established customers or not.

Alvin and his wife stayed in New York five months, until May, then returned to Chicago. In February, 1943, he was drafted into the Army. Meanwhile, Phil Sarfatty, former buyer for the Stevens Hotel (now the Conrad Hilton) in Chicago, a small, thin man of strongly held opinions, took over the Brooklyn office.

The Hudson Avenue building, meanwhile, sprang cracks in

Jacob Cohn, August of 1942.

its walls, worrying the roaster, James Dempsey. Mr. Dempsey, a voluble New Yorker to his fingertips, collared Stan Owens during one of his trips from Chicago and pointed out what to him were telltale signs of coming collapse.

The building or even parts of it could collapse and trap everybody in it, Mr. Dempsey warned, and there was merit to the dire prediction as far as the shape and inner configuration of the building were concerned. Its entrance in front led up one long, thin flight to the building's office and then up another long flight to the packing and shipping room.

Back in Chicago, Mr. Owens told Jacob Cohn, who, characteristically, questioned him further. "Is there any danger?" he asked. Told there might be, Mr. Cohn, concerned about employees' welfare, called for an architect's report on the matter immediately. The architect said that there was no need to evacuate the building, but that Continental should shore up the walls. This would afford adequate protection, the architect said.

The walls were shored up, at a cost of $6,000 or $8,000, and at Jacob Cohn's later suggestion, the building was inspected twice yearly thereafter for further signs of dissolution.

"We want to be sure our employees are safe" was Mr. Cohn's comment on the whole business, instigated as it was by an alert roaster, who was suitably rewarded for his alertness.

The New York operation continued in the doldrums throughout the '40s. Something had to be done, and it was decided Marvin Sommers was the one to do it. One day in 1951, he and Alvin Cohn took a trip to Brooklyn at Jacob Cohn's request.

Mr Sommers, Milwaukee-based sales supervisor for several states, was in the dark about why the trip was being made. He didn't know it, but he was soon to take over the New York sales operation. His first indication was Alvin's telling him he should look for a house in the area. Not even Mr. Sarfatty, the branch manager, knew what was going on. Stanley Owens knew; he had suggested Mr. Sommers as ideal for New York. Jacob Cohn, the master planner of this maneuver, was on his way to Europe.

The Levine brothers, who ran the Brass Rail restaurants and were good friends of Jacob Cohn and good customers, suggested Mr. Sommers try Great Neck, Long Island. A few weeks later, Mr. Sommers made his move from Milwaukee to New York.

He had joined Continental in April, 1943, as a route salesman after selling Van Heusen shirts for Phillip Jones, but only after convincing Jacob Cohn that he could drive a truck and lug coffee into restaurant kitchens. He'd been driving around with boxes of shirt samples, after all, lugging *them* into stores, he explained.

National sales convention, Chicago's Knickerbocker Hotel, 1943.

CONTINENTAL COFFEE CO.
NATIONAL SALES CONVENTION
KNICKERBOCKER HOTEL CHICAGO 1943

He also dropped the name of Walter Belinky, whom he had met three or four years earlier. Mr. Belinky, by then in the Army, had left Continental about the time Alvin Cohn took over New York. Mr. Sommers, thirty years old and experienced, was able to work out with Jacob Cohn the understanding that he would be promoted in due time to a sales management position.

That understanding had already been verified when Mr. Sommers arrived in New York. On his first day of work as coffee salesman to the Big Apple, he stood at 42nd and Lexington wondering where he should start. The pause was momentary.

Off calling on customers, he found the people friendly, their coffee strong, and their coffee-making urns inadequate. He called Jacob Cohn, now back in Chicago from his European trip, and asked for some serpentine-front urns, for these New Yorkers to use in making and serving good, strong Continental coffee.

Mr. Cohn approved a dozen of these for shipment from Continental's urn-making facility to the company's new man on the East Coast. Mr. Sommers then sold or loaned these to customers. Urns sold for $400 in most cases, considerably lower than the market price. The buyer could pay by the week or by pound of coffee bought (a dime extra, upping per-pound price to 45 cents) if he did not want to pay the lump sum up front. Loaning the urn was a concession to New York City practices. The urn-borrower was informed he could keep it as long as he bought Continental coffee.

Coffee, always a high-margin item for restaurants, was selling at a dime a cup in a city with a high dining-out average among its millions of citizens. The new urns helped Continental sales, and in not too long, New York City customers were buying an average of 100 pounds of coffee a week each. This was high even for New York City. In other cities 50 to 65 pounds a week was high.

Sales staff under Mr. Sommers was eventually expanded from five to thirty-five routes, covering Maine to the Carolinas. By 1961 the Brooklyn branch was selling almost 4.3 million pounds of coffee a year. Mr. Sommers had pride in the Continental product and recalls to this day that it was one of the few restaurant coffees on the Eastern Seaboard that labeled its packages. Most were sold in "plain brown wrappers."

Some also were sold, in New York at least, on a kickback basis. That is, buyers (chefs, managers and the like) were guaranteed some sort of under-table return for buying a given brand of coffee. Jacob Cohn and the Continental organization were adamant against such practices.

By 1961 the Brooklyn office had a batch of high-volume, prestige customers. Its "IBM billing machines" billed Washington's Mayflower Hotel, the Brass Rail restaurants in New York and the Somerset Hotel in Boston. Also among its customers were most airlines operating out of New York and Newark airports and plant cafeterias in many of the largest factories on the East Coast, including those of IBM, General Electric and Ford.

A year later, the Brooklyn plant was one of seven Continental roasting operations. The others were in Chicago, Denver, Seattle, Los Angeles, St. Paul and Toledo. With the move to the East had also come the realization that people in different parts of the country had different tastes in coffee. Those in the East liked it heavier, full bodied. Indeed, 90 percent of Continental sales in the East were of WB, the company's best grade of coffee.

In the '50s and '60s in New York Marv Sommers was sales manager. Simon Rice replaced Phil Sarfatty as branch manager in January, 1953. Mr. Rice had come to the U. S. in September, 1938, from his native Germany, fleeing from Nazi persecution.

He met Jacob Cohn at the W&R (for Weiskopf and Rice) Restaurant, a well-known Chicago Loop deli and a Continen-

Continental's East Coast salesmen and managers, early 1950s. National sales manager Walter Belinky is third from left, front row. To his right is East Coast sales manager Marvin Sommers. To Mr. Sommers's right is Brooklyn branch manager Simon Rice.

tal customer to the huge amount of 400 pounds of coffee a week. Simon's uncle, one of the proprietors, introduced him to Mr. Cohn as "my nephew looking for a job."

Mr. Rice, then twenty-five, started at Continental on Nov. 7, 1938, at $60 a month and worked there with time out for military service until August, 1975, when he retired.

Put to work matching invoices (as part of the exhaustive Continental internal controls system), he was assistant controller by the time he left for the Army in October, 1942. After the war, still in the Army, he worked as an interpreter at the Nuremburg war crimes trial, returning to civilian life in April, 1946.

During his time in Chicago before and after military service, Mr. Rice got a flavor of the Continental culture that remains with him to this day. Some little things meant a lot, like the cut-rate (but good) coffee available to employees for as little as $1.03 for five pounds, the company's gifts to employees at Thanksgiving (a turkey) and Christmas ($5 for each year of service) and service awards at the company-subsidized Credit Union dinners.

These annual dinners were major social events for many employees. Awards ranged from the 5-year pin to the 25-year watch and on up to the special 50-year award determined by the chairman — Jacob Cohn or, later, one of his two sons who held the position, Alvin or Robert. Another award, the President's Award, Mr. Rice himself received later, in New York, for hiring and training two particularly productive employees.

Mr. Rice himself was sometimes sent by Mr. Cohn to make a final check on restaurants to whom Continental made cash loans of up to $5,000. He was to see what sort of place the borrower ran, down to the cleanliness of his washrooms. The loan by this time would be in final stages of approval, but if obvious problems arose, it might not be granted. Such loans were made to good customers who were expanding their businesses and thus were incurring added short-term expenses.

Moving to New York, Mr. Rice brought with him the spirit he had imbibed in Chicago. In any event, he helped arrange the first Continental employees' picnic for the New York branch in the summer of 1953, a few months after he arrived as branch manager. Others on the picnic committee were Miss Marian Matteo, a veteran of at least twelve years with the company, Marv Sommers, Jim Dempsey the roaster and Miss B. Sterner.

The affair, held at a place called Schmidt's Farm, drew picnickers from New York, New Jersey, Connecticut and even Philadelphia. Adults and older children played ping-pong, handball and rolling-pin throw. "Small fry" scrambled for pennies and pitched clothespins.

The day's main event was men's baseball, while the ladies played canasta (a popular card game) under the trees. A full-course dinner on the patio, accompanied by music from the juke box, was followed by egg-throwing, bust-the-balloons, and fellows' and girls' footraces. Mike Napolitano and his sister Rose won three prizes, and youngsters played "donkey games" as "proud Daddies" snapped pictures, the employee newsletter *Continental Courier*, reported.

The East Coast operation grew during the '50s and '60s, especially in New Jersey, Connecticut, Maryland, and in the Washington and Philadelphia areas. The plant, now on Long Island, was not big enough to meet the newly increased needs. Continental plant manager Jim McManus and Stanley Owens recommended a new one-story building.

Their eyes turned across the river to New Jersey, where they told a real estate firm to find them some land. The company looked at a new industrial subdivision. The price was right, streets and sewers were in place, the lot size and shape were just right, everything was ready.

But it was a little like being first on the moon: no one else was there yet. Continental would be one of the subdivision's first residents. Better early than never, the company decided, and Continental built there, at Moonachie, N. J., on a 12-acre site. The new plant opened in October, 1965.

Company executives and employees were proud of the new plant, as if with a bouncing baby boy. The Moonachie roasting plant was just what they wanted. Moonachie itself (it's an Indian name) was not far from Newark and was handy to the Midtown and Hudson tunnels and the George Washington bridge.

But times and the company profile changed radically in the next decade, and in August, 1976, Continental sold the Moonachie plant and switched coffee distribution for the East Coast to the Toledo plant. When that was found to be impractical, the company switched East Coast coffee distribution to other distributors. The company was so far removed by then from being mainly a coffee business that it wasn't even distributing all of its own product. Currently twenty to twenty-five companies are distributing Continental coffee.

Another East Coast venture has a history that spans several decades. It's the story of Continental Coffee Company's one and only franchise, in Miami, Florida. It began sometime in the '30s, before the New York move, when Continental sent salesman Morry Koven, brother of Henry Koven, the company's lawyer, to Miami to open up a branch.

Sometime after this operation was under way, Mr. Cohn, hearing things were not going well in Florida, paid a surprise visit. What he saw — two Continental trucks parked near the beach and two route men taking their ease in the Florida sun — confirmed the reports that the financial situation was weak down there.

Disappointed, he told Mr. Koven he was going to shut the operation down. Mr. Koven pleaded with him to keep it going or at least stake him to the credit he needed to keep it going himself. He agreed to do this, on the condition that Mr. Koven buy his green coffee from Continental. Mr. Koven built the business up virtually as his own, finally becoming independent of Continental financing but continuing to use the name Continental Coffee Company of Florida. Mr. Koven ran the company in Florida until 1970, when he sold it to Continental.

6. PITTSBURGH AND TOLEDO

By 1940 Dan Pacini, hired nine years earlier by Walter Belinky, was a district sales manager in Chicago, with five routes under him. He hired and fired, supervised salesmen, serviced his own customers and in general stayed on top of the territory. As a district manager, he also enjoyed "overrights," that is, a share in his district's sales.

But his ears perked up when he heard of salesman's openings in Wheeling, West Virginia, and in beautiful nearby Wisconsin. In either case he would have to go back to route work, selling from his truck, keeping voluminous records and lugging coffee in and out of restaurants.

But what he had in mind was market opportunity, as district manager or not. Wisconsin was beautiful, but Wheeling was close to Pittsburgh, an industrialized city loaded with coffee-drinkers and surrounded by many smaller cities, the kind where Continental had always done very well.

So he went to Wheeling, to take the place of a man who was not doing well. The first thing he did was go out and sell five new restaurants right off the bat. It was Chicago all over again.

In Washington, Pennsylvania, halfway between Wheeling and Pittsburgh, he sold the George Washington Hotel, a 250-pounds-a-week account — five times what was considered a good coffee account in that area. He did it by selling the buyer, who drank a sample that Mr. Pacini brewed and then sold the manager, a Mr. Lippincott, while Mr. Pacini just watched. It was another case of letting the coffee do the talking. The losing competitor was locally based Neff Coffee Co.

Mr. Pacini soon became district manager and at sales meetings was a strong advocate of the taste-test, which he gave regularly to his salesmen. He also stressed the importance of respecting prospective customers' loyalty to the products they were using.

The problem with many salesmen, he said, is that they do not know how to overcome customer reluctance based upon brand loyalty. This was the challenge he loved. Facing it daily gave flavor to everything he did.

As district manager he hired salesmen who were cleancut and dressed neatly, as company policy required. Diners saw them come and go where they were eating; so they had to look good. Mr. Pacini himself wore a derby. So did others. All wore white shirt and tie and a suit and a hat in winter, and in the summer white shirt and slacks.

The company wanted them to feel and be treated like salesmen. They were to look the part of men who could brew coffee for a club manager or maitre d'. At the same time, they had to deliver the goods physically, sometimes in big packages, in all weather.

Within two years after Mr. Pacini came to Wheeling, the U. S. was at war, and the country's commercial life was affected radically. Inter-city, over-the-road trucking, on which Pittsburgh depended for coffee delivered from Chicago, began to show signs of breaking down under wartime strains.

There were failures of equipment, shortages of spare parts and the like. Deliveries from Chicago became a doubtful proposition. Mr. Pacini, by now the Pittsburgh-area sales manager with twenty men under him, complained at a sales meeting at the Schenley Hotel in Pittsburgh. What Pittsburgh needed was its own roasting plant, Mr. Pacini said. His salesmen were in trouble. Without coffee, how could they sell?

It was agreed that the wartime situation called for a Pittsburgh plant. A place was found at 2124 Penn Avenue and Mr. Pacini was told to buy it. The owner was a Philadelphia bank, which played hard to get. Mr. Pacini went to Philadelphia after some fruitless negotiations and made them a final offer of $41,000, telling them to take it or leave it and that he'd be back in a few hours. He came back and the deal was struck.

It was 1943, and Continental Coffee Company opened its third roasting plant, after those in Chicago and in Brooklyn, New York, equipping the new place with Jabez Burns roasting equipment, which was standard at the time.

Sales continued to be Mr. Pacini's area, however. He sold the railroad engine-shop cafeterias in Altoona, Pennsylvania, giving customers the taste test with the cafeteria manager looking on. The losing competitor was Standard Brands, a national operation.

Years later at the Standard Club in Chicago, Mr. Pacini met a Standard Brands executive who remembered him from Altoona. "You're the one who took all that business away from me," said the executive, who could be forgiven for remembering because the order was for a whopping 500 pounds a week.

The Pittsburgh roasting operation lasted until 1949, a year or so after Continental bought a much bigger plant in Toledo. The Toledo operation, located with better access to Detroit, Pittsburgh and other markets, was to serve Continental's postwar expansion far better than the Pittsburgh plant would have served it.

Dan Pacini stayed on in Pittsburgh selling coffee until 1965, when he retired after working half time for two years. Never in his thirty-five years of selling Continental coffee did he waver in his belief in the product and never did he regret the day he sold Walter Belinky on giving him a try at selling it.

Meanwhile, the Pittsburgh plant was looking more and more like the mainly stopgap measure it was to meet the wartime conditions. In 1948 Continental shipped 16.5 million pounds of coffee and $2.5 million worth of allied products to a dozen or more cities from its three plants — in Chicago, Brooklyn and Pittsburgh.

Pittsburgh was clearly the least of these, and when the chance came to roast in a bigger, more centrally located plant, General Manager Stan Owens was ready to jump at it. Toledo was the opportunity — 250 miles from Chicago, 230 from Pittsburgh, 135 from Columbus, 110 from Cleveland, and only 60 from Detroit. A rail center in its own right, Toledo fell in the middle of territory then served by Chicago and Pittsburgh.

Word came from Norman Dessum, district sales manager in Toledo, that Karavan Coffee Company, a major local roaster and distributor, was for sale.

Jacob Cohn, Stan Owens and the company's lawyer, Henry Koven, took a train to Toledo one day in 1948 to cement the transaction, which almost ran aground once the two principal owners got to talking about it face to face.

The Karavan owner, Mr. Brucker, opened the discussion with the request that Mr. Cohn promise to take good care of Mr. Brucker's customers — a request that Mr. Cohn found not only superfluous but mildly insulting as well. He took exception to it on the spot, Mr. Brucker responded in kind, and the whole transaction stood in jeopardy.

Mr. Koven took Mr. Cohn, his client, aside; and the other attorney, an ex-judge named Dunne, took Mr. Brucker aside. Both lawyers explained what the other fellow meant, and soon a calmer mood prevailed. The papers were signed, and Continental had a new coffee plant and sales operation.

Karavan had once sold coffee retail, and the plant size reflected that. It was at least twice the size of Brooklyn and similarly dwarfed Pittsburgh. Much of its space was unused, but was there to be used. And the location was perfect. Stan Owens hurried back to Chicago to decide how Karavan could be used to its full extent.

He huddled with Lou Leichentritt, then a newly hired manager, and the two worked out new coffee routes to fit the new facility. It all fit together nicely.

The plant was run by Harry Gill, Mr. Brucker's brother-in-law, a short, peppy fellow in his sixties. But Mr. Owens intended to use the unused capacity, with the goal of tripling or quadrupling output. In due time, therefore, the services of a younger man were judged necessary. Mr. Owens looked to Pittsburgh, where Leonard Giunto had been hired during the previous year to help manage the Pittsburgh office. He looked to Pittsburgh for two reasons: its days were numbered as a roasting operation, and it was doing well. The Toledo operation could use an injection of Pittsburgh spirit and expertise.

Mr. Giunto, a job-hungry army veteran who had done clerical work before the war, answered a Continental ad in the "female help wanted" section. He was at the Pittsburgh plant for an interview on a Saturday when Jacob Cohn was in town for a sales meeting. Mr. Cohn met him and liked him. He passed muster in other respects as well, and was hired that day.

He worked first in office management, then in sales and production. Pittsburgh had two roasting machines and a small staff. His work included developing sales bulletins, copies of which he sent regularly to Chicago.

In July of 1949, Mr. Giunto made the move to Toledo as office manager, after discussing it with Dan Pacini. Mr. Pacini had hired Mr. Giunto, for one thing. In addition, Mr. Giunto, who was not yet married, had close family ties in Pittsburgh; and Mr. Owens did not want to pressure him to make the move. He preferred to present him with the opportunity and let him decide.

Mr. Giunto decided to make the move. But there was a hitch. He was engaged. The move to Toledo meant a period of commuting to Pittsburgh on weekends to visit his intended, Dorothy, who became his wife and the mother of their three children.

When he arrived, he found Robert Cohn, Jacob Cohn's son, who left shortly thereafter for Brazil. Norm Dessum was district sales manager. Jim Chengges, later a district sales manager, was the Toledo route salesman. Those were the days of frequent product promotions. If a restaurant operator bought a certain amount of chocolate syrup, he was given a discount rate on sundae glasses. If he bought so much iced tea, he would pay less for a big spigot-equipped iced-tea dispensing jar or even get one free.

Toledo moved ahead of New York in coffee roasting and distribution. Even in the '50s and '60s, after several other plants were operating for Continental around the country, Toledo held on to its Number Two position behind Chicago.

In addition to coffee roasted in Toledo, the Toledo office distributed seven or eight trailer-loads a week of dressings, puddings and spices from Chicago, not to mention urns and other equipment. Indeed, the branch, which Mr. Giunto headed almost from his arrival, became Continental's top distributor of allied (non-coffee) products.

Through the office came 1,600 to 1,700 invoices a day, which compared well enough with Chicago's 2,000 a day. All were processed by hand. Each order, mailed or dropped off at day's end by salesmen for delivery a week later, went to the office's order desk. There a woman priced and extended and added the amounts.

The orders then went to the billing clerk sitting at an IBM typewriter with a carbon feed for invoices. These she typed. Invoices and orders then went to another clerk for checking one against the other. Then they went to another, who gathered like items on a recap sheet.

This recap sheet went to the order-filler in the plant. This order-filler used it to compile the "salesman's load" for the day. Then the recap sheet was sent to the warehouse with a set of billed invoices.

Here the merchandise, now gathered on a four-wheel dolly,

was checked to see that it matched both order and invoice. In case of discrepancy, the clerk would use the order copies as checks on the recap.

The merchandise, now checked and double-checked, went to the shipping department, where it was sent off with a set of invoices, including the re-order copy. The salesman arrived at the truck dock at the end of each day, around dinner time, there to pick up his load for delivery the next day.

In making his deliveries, at virtually the same time of the same day every week, he might find the customer had over-ordered. In any event, he had to keep his inventory up to date in view of additions and deletions and he had to make a cash report in addition to that. He remitted cash daily to Toledo, where the cashier and inventory clerk checked it. If the amount was incorrect, he would receive an "error notice." The cashier and inventory clerk kept a record of this.

The whole business was quite detailed. Communications with Chicago or anywhere else outside Toledo were by first class surface (not air) mail, almost never by telephone or special delivery. Air mail was used somewhat less rarely.

Messrs. Owens and Giunto periodically discussed possible better ways of controlling the order and fulfillment process. Mr. Giunto at length ran across a copying machine, one of the first of its kind, which he used to copy orders. But this put the burden of deciphering salesmen's handwriting on too many people, and they had to return to the services of the typist, who presumably was an expert in such matters.

Then, following Chicago's lead, they moved to an IBM tab-card calculator, for use in billing. This eliminated typing errors and made it easier to analyze sales, to produce a sort of scorecard on what sold and what didn't.

Fifty-two salesmen worked out of the Toledo office in eleven states. It was the biggest-volume branch outside Chicago, with six district sales managers overseeing the fifty-two. In the whole process of taking orders, processing them at the Toledo

Meeting in Toledo of Cleveland, Detroit and Toledo salesmen, October 30, 1954. Alvin Cohn and his son Lee are in the front, middle. Others include Leonard Giunto, far left in the front, and Detroit sales manager Al Marans to his right; Toledo sales manager J. G. Chengges and Dr. Jack Bloom to Alvin Cohn's right, and Toledo salesman Norm Dessum on the far right, front.

office and filling and delivering them, timing was critical. Mr. Giunto as branch manager was often at the plant up to midnight seeing the work was completed. The mails, not the telephone wires, which were rarely used, were full of correspondence with the salesmen.

In the office itself were probably thirty people. Chicago had more people but did more work, including companywide payroll, commissions, accounting, and government reports. Toledo couldn't use temporaries because its work was not standardized, but it still gave Chicago a run for its money in efficiency and low overhead.

The warehouse manager kept daily records in a loose-leaf notebook, keeping up inventory and re-ordering from Chicago. The salesman received his invoices in cartons marked with an "X". If the invoices did not arrive, he had to call Toledo by telephone — an extreme measure that reflected the magnitude of the problem. Without the invoices, the salesman could not know which goods went to which customers, The added expense of the phone call made this a "bad, bad" alternative, in Mr. Giunto's words.

The five-story building Continental bought from Karavan was not efficient, but luckily the state of Ohio decided to send a new expressway through it. At first, Jacob Cohn was not happy about the condemnation for the sake of Interstate 75. He like multistory buildings and saw nothing wrong with the one they had.

But he was eventually convinced that they had no choice in the matter and that it was good to move into a building they would build for their purposes. This was the first one Continental had built this way. Bigger than the original one, it was built at 3100 Summit Street in Toledo.

The *Continental Courier* for November, 1953, pictures the new building in process of construction and comments that at the old location it was "not unusual to see a house moving down the street" as it was moved from the path of the interstate. The Courier found it "a little ghostly" around the old plant those days, and expected Continental to be the last to leave.

The old building was in a residential neighborhood, and housewives complained about chaff (coffee bean flakes) which flew off during the quenching of the roast. This chaff would collect on clothes put out to dry, much to the homemakers' chagrin. It also would collect in the building's gutters. One night it caught fire. Mr. Giunto was aroused from sleep and came to find firemen dousing the blaze.

As general manager in the '40s and '50s, Stan Owens made frequent trips to Toledo. He would often leave his office just after the rush hour in Chicago and driving would make it to Toledo late at night. Then he would be ready for business the next day.

On one trip as he took his customary walk through the plant, he was stopped by an employee, "the sweet but timid" Mary Paulus, who had been promoted from coffee packaging to the spice department but wasn't happy there. The work was all right, she told him, but it was lonely in the spice department. Would he ask her boss, Chuck Edmiston, about it?

She was doing a great job, said Mr. Edmiston, who was reluctant to move her. "She'll quit if you keep her there," said Mr. Owens. Mr. Edmiston didn't want that to happen; so he moved Mrs. Paulus and the whole spice department, just a few employees, next to her friends in coffee packaging. Thus Mrs. Paulus was once more happy at her work.

7. SELLING COFFEE TO THE NATION

The Continental route salesman of forty years ago, unlike salesmen for other coffee companies, was paid commission and not a straight salary. This provided him the incentive to work hard and sell more coffee and allied products. He did not work by the hour or day but by the amount of coffee and "allieds" sold. The harder he worked, the more money he earned.

The new salesman was put on salary — $60 to $75 a week depending on his territory. Big cities paid the most and small towns the least. When a man opened ten new accounts which bought for twelve consecutive weeks, he went on full commission, which allowed him to earn considerably more than the original $60 or $75.

He also got a bonus for every new account. These new accounts were figured from the beginning of his time with Continental. Thus from the start, he was working for new-account bonuses, though these were not paid until twelve weeks of sales were recorded. He continued to receive bonuses for additional new accounts for as long as he worked for Continental.

At the same time, the salesman was penalized for losing an account. The bonus already received would be deducted from future new-account bonuses (not from commissions, however). Otherwise, the thinking went, what would the salesman have to lose if an account lapsed?

For Continental salesmen a new account meant more money. For other coffee salesmen, it meant only more work. It meant he kept his job too, of course, but Continental salesmen were expected to think beyond that minimum achievement. The Continental salesman, in short, was in business for himself, in partnership with the company.

When at sales meetings there were complaints about this or that, the district sales manager would tell the men, "You're in business for yourself." Most salesmen started their day at 7 A.M. and worked until 6 P.M. or 7 P.M. Some worked even later. If a salesman quit at 4 P.M., this was his business, as long as he did well. He might work his head off, as many if not most did, because he was ambitious and energetic. It was up to him. The incentives were there.

Most lived on the weekly draw, saving the monthly commission check or spending it on bigger-ticket items. If a man made an extra $5,000 a year on commissions, beyond his normal living expenses, he was doing well. The top Continental salesman in Fremont, Ohio, at lunch one day with Stan Owens pointed out the town's bank president eating at the same restaurant and told Mr. Owens that he, the salesman, made more than the bank president. Mr. Owens did not find that hard to believe.

Sales techniques took many forms, some of which we have seen already in the accounts of the Davis brothers and Dan Pacini. Invention knew few limits when a Continental man stormed the fortress of a restaurateur's allegiance to a competitor's coffee.

The taste test was the most important tool, of course. But veteran salesman Marvin Sommers also used a chart he called a "line of standardization" on which he drew the categories into which various brands fell, much as canned goods salesmen did. There were dozens of other techniques used as well. "Once I had a buyer sitting in front of me, I could do it," Mr. Sommers said.

The inventive salesman or district sales manager (DSM) gave out lighters, playing cards, cuff links and the like at Christmas, always with a Continental emblem on them. There was a coffee-bean-shaped tie clasp and a card that went with it that said, "Compliments of Continental Coffee Co.—America's leading coffee to the foodservice industry."

There was a coffee-bean tie pin and a table-top lighter five inches high and shaped like a coffee pot and playing cards that read on the flip side, "Good coffee like good manners pays in popularity." DSMs Bernard Pippenger, in Indianapolis, and Merton Mack, in Decatur, especially liked these means of getting through prospects' defenses. A Zippo pocket lighter, "the original windproof lighter," had a coffee-pot logo on its side.

Sales were "belly to belly," as Jacob Cohn reminded his advertising agency, but there was "image" advertising nonetheless in the 1940s, in trade magazines. As far as that goes, Continental's spic-and-span brown and green panel trucks with their bright, easily read metal lettering, were rolling ads on city and suburban streets.

There was a direct-mail campaign too, and even a little retail selling of Continental coffee in restaurants. On the counter next to the cash register, for instance, the diner might find a bag to buy on his way out, the taste of good coffee still fresh in his memory.

There was the national restaurant show in Chicago, attended by 70,000 foodservice people, with up to 400 booths. Continental always had its own booths, where it served its coffee with doughnuts free. As restaurateurs came for a cup, a Continental photographer would take their pictures, which then were sent to Continental sales managers who passed them on to the salesman for giving to the customer or prospect — a nice touch that might make the man more receptive next time a taste test was suggested. The district sales manager would later check with the salesman to see what results were achieved from this effort.

Then there were sales aids provided by the home office, on Ontario Street from the late 1920s to 1957, when it was moved to Clybourn Avenue. At the center of this for much of this time was Walter Belinky, who spent many weeks a year on the road with salesmen and became a student of salesmanship.

Mr. Belinky's booklet, "On Overcoming Objections," became more or less expected, if not required reading for salesmen. His sales promotion letters, as one explaining the grinder plan already described, became a standard tool. From 1948 on, he had the help of Gerald Ryan, who served first as personal secretary to Mr. Cohn and later wrote sales brochures and letters.

When Mr. Ryan arrived in 1948, at Ontario Street, conditions were crowded, and he often had to evict one of the outside auditors from his desk in order to have room to work. Coffee was 39 cents a pound, sales were $12 million a year.

Mr. Belinky and Mr. Ryan developed an honest relationship which sometimes proceeded in a roundabout manner. Mr. Belinky's typist, Florence Weinstein, found her written work consistently displeasing or rather, insufficiently pleasing to Mr. Belinky, who covered it with written corrections. She asked Mr. Ryan to intercede.

Mr. Ryan, who respected her work, came at Mr. Belinky with a disarming: "Walter, we try to keep you happy because you're a genius." Mr. Belinky, catching the irony, smiled. "But Florence is very good at what she does. Why are you marking up her work?"

Mr. Ryan had saved some samples of Florence's work. "I have asked her to make mistakes," he said, producing sheets full of corrections by Mr. Belinky, "so that you can enjoy making the changes." Mr. Belinky got the message and thereafter went easier on her.

The two of them worked at educating the salesmen, showing them how to push products. For their chili con carne, Mr. Belinky concocted the slogan, "Chilly weather is chili weath-

Robert Cohn and Stanley Owens are shown in the mid-'50s encouraging restaurant and other foodservice operators to serve a "generous cup" of coffee, during a time of coffee price increases which tempted them to skimp. Continental sold these oversize cups for operators to display as a sign of their policy.

er," for instance. They would instruct a salesman to enter a customer's restaurant wearing a teabag on his lapel or to bring a mayonnaise sample, lay it on the counter and wait for the customer to pick up. In each case, Mr. Belinky and Mr. Ryan would tell the salesman what to say to stimulate tea or mayonnaisse sales, as the case might have been.

They showed the salesmen how to perform the brewing demonstration, for instance. This was when coffee was ninety percent of sales. There was a way to ask a diner what he or she thought so as to lessen chances of a negative response. They were not to ask, "Which did you like better?" but "Which has more coffee flavor?" If the diner said the coffee was bitter, the salesman would say, "It's natural," meaning

The Continental Twin Junior Urn featuring the automatic tea tank used in the '30s, '40s, and 50s.

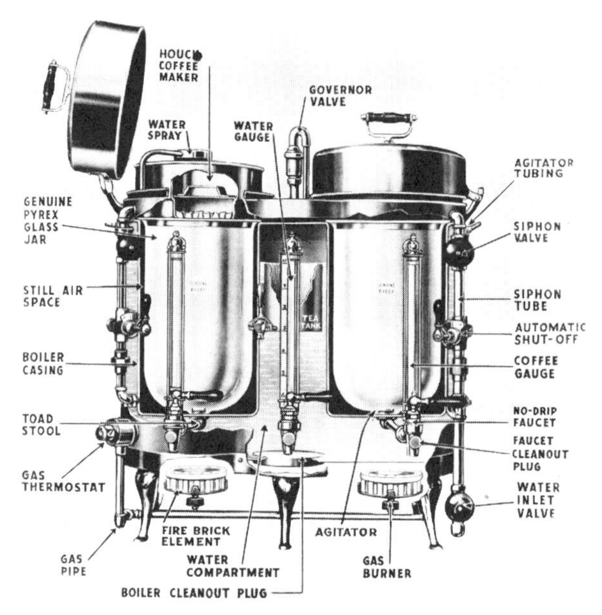

The inside of a twin urn.

this coffee was the real stuff and maybe you're not used to the real stuff.

Route salesmen had to get used to the unexpected — late loads, vehicle breakdowns, customer equipment problems and other emergencies. In a sense, an impossible combination was asked of them — loading trucks, keeping inventory, returning mistakenly delivered merchandise or equipment needing repair, seeing that restaurant urns were clean, and on top of all that, the paper work.

Some stand out in Mr. Ryan's memory. Kenny Babb, a district sales manager in Champaign, Illinois, was an "artist" when it came to cleaning urns and showing restaurant operators how to do it, Mr. Ryan recalls. On the street at 6 A.M., the six-foot-three-inch Mr. Babb, a former Air Corps captain, was eager to please customers but discovered limits once in Rockford, Illinois, before he went to Champaign. One called with a problem at 2 A.M., waking him four hours before he was to start his work day. The coffee machine was not working, the customer informed Mr. Babb, who got himself out of bed and made his way to the restaurant. There he found the plug pulled and promptly told the customer's wife what he thought of such foolishness.

Bernard Pippenger, in Indianapolis, defended his men no matter what, even when Stan Owens complained vigorously about inventory errors or driving accidents. Merton Mack in Decatur, Illinois, a fast-talking, alert perfectionist, was the only DSM who checked regularly to see that his men used the selling guide provided by the main office. His men were neat, clean-cut, young-looking. Mack himself had been a haberdasher and looked the part.

Dan Pacini, Merton Mack, Bernard Pippenger, Bob Campbell, Eugene Irwin and Joe Davis by their sales inventiveness and energy contributed mightily to the company's success. Mr. Pippenger, for instance, ran sales contests for his men and paid the winners several hundred dollars out of his own pocket.

This gathering in Chicago in the 1950s included: *(STANDING): far left,* Aaron A. Good; *4th from left,* Gene Irwin; *6th,* Kenneth Babb; *8th,* Norm Dessum; and *at the right end,* Stanley Owens, Alvin and Jacob Cohn and Walter Belinky; *(SITTING): far left,* Marvin Sommers; *3rd from left,* Merton Mack; *4th,* Dan Pacini; *second from right and far right respectively,* Gerald Ryan and Bernard Pippenger.

Mr. Campbell, in Cincinnati, held sales meetings at his own expense.

Now and then one of the veterans had a neophyte to contend with. One of them was Joe Harjung, now in charge of shortening production on the West Coast, who worked with and for crack salesman Harry Davis on Chicago's Near North Side, in the nightclub district. Mr. Harjung suffered in silence for a time while Mr. Davis put the pressure on him. Finally he called the older man on it. Mr. Davis was philosophical about it: "I just wanted to see if you could take it," he said.

Pressures abounded for the young man new on the job, ambitious and eager but inexperienced. Once Mr. Harjung, still a shipping room employee, subbed on short notice for a relief salesman who had fallen and broken his arm in the middle of a day.

At Alvin Cohn's request, Mr. Harjung picked up the salesman's truck and invoices at the hospital where he had gone for treatment and finished his route for him. Returning late to the sales room at Ontario Street, he asked the only salesman still around the place where to put the cash and checks from the day's sales and was told "on top of the safe."

The man was referring to a slot on top of the safe through which the money could be slipped so that no one but the cashier could retrieve it. But there was a plain wire basket on top of the safe, and Mr. Harjung unfortunately assumed that was where the money went. He put it there in an envelope with his paper work and left for the day, innocent but about to become sadder and wiser in a few hours.

That was when he returned to work the next day and was asked where the money was. On top of the safe, he said, in the wire basket. That's not where it was at all, however, and Mr. Harjung was grilled by Mr. Belinky and Mr. Owens until they were satisfied he hadn't pocketed the receipts.

At the plant on Ontario Street, Mr. Harjung and others worked in the part of a coffee sales operation that customers didn't see — packing and shipping. The coffee sold in Chicago and the Midwest came out of Ontario Street.

Winter snow presented its own challenges to coffee delivery, needless to say. On one very snowy Sunday, Stan Owens took a call from Jacob Cohn asking him to go to Ontario Street and pick up some coffee and salad dressing for a major customer — Ashkenaz Restaurant, a Rogers Park deli which bought 400 pounds of coffee a week. Mr. Owens lived fairly near the Ontario Street plant and was heading in the direction of Ashkenaz anyhow that afternoon to visit relatives with his wife.

Thanks to snow tires he had on his car, he was able to drive to the plant, where he picked up three cases of coffee and some dressing, and then to Rogers Park. Snow tires or not, parking was a problem, and he had to lug the first case of coffee through knee-deep snow a half-block to the deli. There he encountered the owner, who showed no particular interest in having one of his employees help carry the rest of the cases.

Stan Owens's experience with the snow tires stayed with him, and for the following winter he purchased them for Continental's Chicago fleet. The Continental trucks were the first food vehicles in Chicago to have snow tires, which made all the difference in and out of snow — in it because they gave as good traction as chains, out of it because they didn't have to be removed when the snow melted.

Many the driver who had to stop in the middle of an early spring day to get rid of the now worse than useless chains, or worse yet, drive back to the garage to have them removed. No more of that, once Continental had snow tires.

One year a big snowstorm uncovered a bit of heroism in the Continental crew. As the storm got worse, most were sent home early. Miller King stayed on, however. He was a mechanic in the garage on Clybourn Avenue. It was his job to keep the area plowed with the aid of a jeep-like vehicle.

When one driver, Cas Miller, called in from the Southwest Side, stalled and sick with the flu, Mr. King found him and brought him back. Mr. King also helped other drivers that day and then stayed all night at the plant, plowing driveways and otherwise helping to keep the operation going. He was remembered for that, as he was for his courtesy to the drivers, who depended so heavily on the mechanics.

When Mr. King, who was black and thus vulnerable to discriminatory real estate practices, found himself in the market for a house in the mid-1950s, Jacob Cohn asked Mr. Owens to accompany him on his search. Mr. Owens did so, helping to negotiate the price and seeing that Mr. King received a credit-union loan and a cash advance on what he had accumulated through the profit-sharing fund.

Later, when the company closed its garage at Clybourn, Mr. King left its employ. He eventually bought a hardware store, near 76th Street and Stony Island Avenue on the South Side, which he currently operates.

Another employee who left the company under quite different circumstances was Lester Mower, a successful route salesman in Toledo. Such was his record, in fact, that Jacob Cohn spotted him for an outstanding performer and offered him the district sales manager's position in Cleveland.

Mr. Mower liked the idea but could not persuade his wife to make the move. Mr. Cohn, pressing the point, came to Toledo with Mrs. Cohn and took the Mowers out to dinner. Before the meal was over, he and Mrs. Cohn had persuaded Mrs. Mower that the move to Cleveland was a good idea.

Off went the Mowers to Cleveland, where after a few months Mrs. Mower reconsidered the matter and said she wanted to go back to Toledo. Again Mr. Cohn personally intervened, this time visiting the Mowers' Cleveland home. Again he persuaded Mrs. Mower, or so he thought. In a week, however, Mr. Mower called to say his wife had gone back to Toledo. He returned also and resumed route sales work there. He later left the company to go into the restaurant business on his own, where he did well.

The Mower episode was one of the few cases where Jacob Cohn misjudged a situation involving an employee transfer. Ever solicitous of a wife's reactions, he did all he thought he could in this case to meet her objections, but it didn't work.

In the 1950s, the company changed coffee bags as an economy measure. The bleached white paper which had been used for the top-grade "WB" blend became too expensive; so at Jacob Cohn's direction the company switched to the kraft (brown-paper) bag used for the lesser brands.

Alvin Cohn and several district sales managers worried about the change and let Jacob Cohn know their concerns. He told them: "We are giving our customers value, not the color of the bag. If we are good salesmen, we can explain to our customers that the blend is the same, that they are getting the same coffee at the same price, thanks to our using a different bag."

As follow-through on this advice, the company sent letters to customers to explain the seemingly small change that nonetheless was the sort that came into the customers' daily awareness. A few complained, but in general the conversion to a different bag was well received.

Another change, the decision in the early 1960s to service national accounts, affected salesmen directly. These accounts — A.R.A. Services, Canteen Corporation and other national operations — bought more but at lower prices and thus at lower salesmen's commissions.

The company as a whole did well with national accounts, but individual branch earnings did not always reflect the extra handling and paperwork, since a branch might have only one or two units of such an account and thus not enough volume to justify the increased effort. For a number of years, in fact, branches who serviced national accounts were subsidized at the suggestion of Mr. Ryan at the home office. It was the unusual case of something being good for the company but not for the branch, and the company acted accordingly.

Meanwhile, Continental was faced with the need for controls as they had to be applied to a national sales operation. Many were involved in the company's switch from the list-making and ledger-keeping by hand of the '30s and '40s to computerized recordkeeping.

But one employee more than others led the way. He was Earl Edwards, who joined the company in January of 1948, and left in May of 1973. Mr. Edwards, a high-school graduate from Cicero, Illinois, with only a little bit of college, took up computer work with zest and probably a bit of genius.

When he came to Continental, he had done a number of things, including delivering milk in horsedrawn wagons and in "Difco" electric trucks. He had re-enlisted after a stint in the military in order to escape the rush for civilian jobs after the war. He joined Continental's salesman's inventory department (and thus was part of the early controls process) and in early '50s volunteered to work with its new tabulating machines — the 402, 403 and 407 IBM models. He took classes in the use of these machines in 1952 at the "Training Within Industry" Foundation in Chicago.

When IBM computers themselves were introduced at Continental, a man named Don Woolsey was recommended to Continental by IBM to supervise their use. After about a year, Mr. Woolsey left Continental to move to California. When he left, Mr. Edwards volunteered again and was put in charge of the company's computers.

It was a big order. Continental was on the verge of a huge conversion. Mr. Edwards took computer courses from IBM in their Chicago school and after that, in 1962, in Endicott, New York, as part of a group whom IBM flew to its classes on the IBM "executive flight." Continental's Lou Leichentritt was part of this group.

The big company changeover came in the early '60s, when Mr. Edwards with the help of a crew of traveling technicians made the switch at Continental facilities, working long hours on weekends, sometimes nonstop. Key to the operation at the Chicago base were Dolores Hoyer and her sister Laverne Rice.

On one weekend Mr. Edwards and his family, who came along for the ride, flew 2,200 miles in the company airplane, making a dozen or so stops. At each stop, Mr. Edwards's family would be put off the plane, and the local Continental people would come aboard for a meeting about how to convert their procedures. It was how things were done in the days before conference calls and videoconferencing.

The discussion on this trip was about use of optical readers in automated ordering. Other trips had to do with actual installations in Toledo, Minneapolis, Seattle, Houston and other Continental cities. In all this, Mr. Edwards, the one in charge, was known for getting down to the actual installation work with his men.

On one occasion in New Jersey, the installation crew was in an auto accident from which they continued to the plant, bruised and limping, and worked on the project until 3 A.M.

Mr. Edwards was based at Clybourn Avenue in Chicago from 1957, when that plant opened. At Clybourn, in fact, he and his crew worked "around the clock" one weekend to install the new system. He left Continental from that location sixteen years later and after a few months consulting work for the company opened a fishing resort in Northern Wisconsin.

He continues to go to school on a need-to-know basis, as he did when at Continental, but now it is for anything from real estate practices to automotive repair. "It keeps my mind going," he says.

8. SEATTLE AND WHAT FOLLOWED

In 1953 Continental took a great leap westward with the purchase of a Seattle, Washington, coffee company that sold under the brand name Royal Corona. This was the Commercial Importing Company, which had been founded in 1885 by a Chicagoan, John Shaw. Mr. Shaw had started in the coffee business in Chicago, selling door to door, and then had moved to Seattle.

The purchase was made after contacts with representatives of Mr. Shaw himself, then in the last year of his life, and later with representatives of his widow. Sometime in 1952, Blythe and Company, the investment firm, contacted Jacob Cohn for Mr. Shaw and informed him that Mr. Shaw's firm was for sale. Blythe apparently knew of Continental through common banking contacts.

Mr. Cohn sent his two sons, Robert and Alvin, to Seattle to meet Mr. Shaw, who unfortunately and unexpectedly turned up not available. The brothers settled for lunch with a Blythe man and the coffee company's auditor, who at one point suggested they fly to Alaska for dinner. But the two brothers excused themselves and returned to Chicago, chalking up the trip to experience.

Within a year of that trip, however, John Shaw died and Jacob Cohn was again contacted, this time by his own bank, Chicago's Continental. Continental Bank had been contacted by Frank Jerome, president of the First National Bank of Seattle, who was trustee of Mr. Shaw's estate. Was Continental Coffee Company interested in the Shaw company?

Continental was interested and made a modest but successful bid. Somewhat to the Cohns' surprise, Mr. Shaw's widow awarded her husband's company to them, reportedly because she was impressed with its profit-sharing system. She apparently regretted that her late husband's company had no such program.

The deal closed, things began to go wrong, however. Local prejudices were held against these "Easterners from Chicago." More than that, there was sabotage. Customers began to complain about the coffee. The coffee was bitter one shipment, too weak the next, then just right the next. One major restaurant operator collected samples in a big glass apothecary jar and showed it to Stanley Owens, who was coordinating the Seattle purchase.

The coffee appeared through the glass jar in several shades, having been roasted to varying degrees of lightness and heaviness. Mr. Owens called Chicago and asked the company's expert taster, Bill Meyer, to come out and help him. Mr. Meyer was shown the jar full of multicolored coffee and began to nose around.

He discovered that the man who did the roasting, a holdover from the previous ownership, was roasting too much, not enough or just right, depending on what day it was and who knows what else. In his tours of the plant, Mr. Meyer also saw a packing department employee slip anise into the coffee. There was more than one way to sabotage a roast.

There were other problems. Mr. Owens found controls lacking to an alarming degree. No records were kept of merchandise shipped, and salesmen were free to keep some invoices and pocket receipts. Being free to do it, they did, as Mr. Owens verified when he told a Royal Corona salesman in Tacoma about the new set of controls being instituted.

Jacob Cohn at the Clybourn plant site, 1957.

"I quit," the man said. He admitted he was keeping some of the sales money but said he couldn't live on his Royal Corona salary. He was urged to reconsider. The company promised to make up what he would lose once the new system was in operation.

Indeed, the pay was low and the company had no incentive system such as Continental salesmen had been enjoying for decades. With changes like these, Continental managed not to lose the Royal Corona sales force, which might otherwise have left for greener pastures once controls were instituted.

Six months or so later, once the area's growth potential was ascertained, two Continental veterans were sent to Seattle from other locations. Walter Struck, the new office manager, came from Toledo, where he had been assistant branch manager under Leonard Giunto after a stint in green coffee buying in Chicago under Bill Meyer. Jim Wykoff, the new sales manager, came from Champaign, Illinois, where he was district sales manager after working as a route salesman.

Their performance in Seattle helped make the operation a success and encouraged Continental to mount similar efforts in Denver, Minneapolis and elsewhere. Indeed, Seattle was the first important move by Continental in its coffee expansion.

It was much farther from Chicago than any previous move, for one thing — seven to ten hours flying time compared to three or four hours driving to Toledo. Neither Pittsburgh nor New York was new territory for Continental. Jacob Cohn for decades went regularly to New York, where the green coffee brokers' offices were located; and Pittsburgh was already proven route-sales territory before a plant was located there.

The New York move in 1939 was trail-blazing, it is true, in that it required the company's first substantial capital outlay since the move to Ontario Street in 1927. But the New York experience was nothing to whet the Continental appetite for further expansion. Arriving with only one customer to speak of — Dario Toffenetti and his world's fair concession — the firm had to struggle for a decade or more.

Seattle, on the other hand, notwithstanding early experience of dirty tricks from the opposition, started Continental on national coffee expansion in the '50s and '60s just as the Keil acquisition in Billings, Montana, was to start them on full-line expansion at the end of the '60s. The Seattle acquisition did this by giving the Cohns a sense of what they could do with their own people far from home.

Much closer to home, Continental took a step into another kind of coffee expansion, namely retail selling, from which it later retreated. This was its move into retail selling in the Chicago area with its purchase in 1954 of the Thomas J. Webb Coffee Company.

The Webb plant was across Ontario Street from the Continental plant. Thomas Webb Sexton, its chief executive, and Stanley Owens used to meet regularly in Otto's Pie Shop, a restaurant run by a big taciturn man who made great pies. Otto's was across the street also. One day Mr. Sexton asked Mr. Owens if Continental might want to buy Thomas J. Webb Company.

Webb's radio commercials featuring "Mortimer" being told by his mother, "Don't forget the Thomas J. Webb coffee," had made it well known. The company enjoyed a number of good sales years but had not followed up on this success and was losing market share to the national brands. This is when Continental bought it. The deal was made in a downtown meeting that took less than an hour.

The Webb company had been founded in the 1890s by a politician who ran for office and bought ad space on cable cars before election day to thank people for voting for him. But he lost the election and ran the ads instead for his coffee. The ads said, "Coffee so good I put my name on it."

Under Continental the Webb company did well. Sales rose from 600,000 to 5,000,000 pounds a year in five years, and the company rose from sixteenth to second place in Chicago-area retail sales.

But problems arose when a retail giant came to Chicago with a virtual giveaway plan with which Continental's Webb could not compete. This was Folger Coffee Company with its "mountain-brewed" coffee. Folger "brought a mountain to Chicago" in the shape of free coupons, assaulting the market and leaving Thomas J. Webb and also McLaughlin's Manor House, another major local coffee retail distributor, reeling. Unwilling to take a loss in Chicago such as the major national companies were willing to take for a time, Continental decided to get out of retail once and for all and in 1960 sold Webb to Butternut Foods.

Meanwhile, in 1957 Continental moved out of the Ontario

At the Clybourn plant site, 1957. Jacob Cohn is second from left, standing. To his right are Stanley Owens, Mrs. Cohn, Robert Cohn and William Meyer. In the front row, beginning second from left, are Harold Murphy, Dr. Jack Bloom and James McManus.

Street plant to newly built quarters three times its size at 2550 North Clybourn Avenue. The move was virtually dictated by space needs and was being considered regardless of the expressway that was coming through and would force them out of Ontario Street. Stan Owens negotiated for the land while James McManus, vice-president-manufacturing, drew up designs which were based on storage and coffee-roasting needs. Mr. McManus had joined the company in 1948 as Ontario Street superintendent and had shortly been made general superintendent of all four Continental plants at the time. In 1957 he was vice-president-manufacturing.

There was no time to waste, and none was wasted. The land was bought and the plant, 120,000 square feet, was built in six months — a single-story building except for the three-story "tower" for roasting and packing coffee. The old plant, on the other hand, was five stories, with 10-foot ceilings. Storage problems abounded. Deliveries had to be made four or five times a day of materials that couldn't be stored, including office materials.

The new place, thanks to its 20-foot-high racks of "pallets" which could be moved in and out with big fork trucks, permitted storage of thirty to sixty days inventory and supplies. A two- to four-hour supply would be kept at floor level, but the rest was accessible without disturbing what was underneath. Thus the new plant allowed storage of goods anywhere in the warehouse area, any of it available in three or four minutes.

The fork trucks were at the heart of this effort. Anticipating the move, Continental looked over the field and narrowed its choice to two brands of pretty much the same price. That's when the company had its fork truck tug-o'-war at the International Amphitheatre on the South Side, in which the final two, each driven by a Continental employee, pulled away at each other. The one that won the big pull — a first in materials-handling equipment annals, says Mr. McManus — was

Continental's choice, and hands down at that. The winner pulled the other one "all over the place," Mr. McManus recalls. In addition to the fork truck, there were the electric scooters, also new in Clybourn, which order-fillers rode or led around the plant.

The move itself from Ontario was a symphony-like cooperation of employees that began at mid-afternoon on a Friday and ended at noon on Sunday, with the new plant opening for business as usual on Monday at 7 A.M. This meant moving everything, but not just to loading docks, of course. Office employees met their boxed files and followed them to their new offices and desks. Anything that ran had to be installed and turned on. "Quite a few" suppliers of machinery and the like came to watch as thirty to forty trailer loads arrived and were unloaded and the whole place was set up.

Guides were placed at the doors and inside the plant on Monday, and signs were distributed throughout the plant, so that people could be directed to their work places. Monday's work went without a hitch, with no time lost.

The new place also acquired some new coffee-bag wrapping machines. When Mr. McManus arrived in 1948, it took ten to fifteen women, each lifting a bag by hand to a spout, to fill and wrap a dozen or fifteen bags of coffee a minute. Then came the "Stokeswrap" machines with which four women did fifteen a minute, six months after Mr. McManus came to the company. Then less than a year after the move to Clybourn, came the "Hesser" machine, German-made in Stuttgart, where Mr. McManus went, Berlitz lessons completed, to supervise its redesigning for use in coffee packing (from its original use, packing sugar). The Hesser machine not only filled bags automatically; it made and printed the bags as well. Now two women could do sixty bags a minute. Hesser machines, at $80,000 apiece, were bought also for Continental's Toledo and New Jersey plants.

About a year after the move to Clybourn, a new coffee

roasting machine was added as well — the Probat roaster, which reduced moisture loss and thus weight loss during roasting. The Jabez Burns roaster, standard in the industry to that time, lost 15% of green coffee weight during roasting. The new Probat lost only 8%. A Probat was gotten for Clybourn Avenue to supplement its eight Jabez Burns roasters, and another was bought for New Jersey, where five Burns roasters continued to be used.

Meanwhile, about the time Continental sold Thomas J. Webb, it took to the coffee expansion trail again, acquiring the Spray Coffee & Spice Co., in Denver. Spray's customers included some of the best in town — the Brown Palace, the Broadmoor Hotel in Colorado Springs, and the Cosmopolitan Hotel. Its owner, Col. Richard Pool, wanted to travel. He also wanted a job for his son.

Stan Owens, sent by Jacob Cohn to negotiate the purchase, spent most of a morning with the colonel at the Brown Palace until the colonel finally said he was satisfied. "I talked so long to see what kind of people you were," he told Mr. Owens. Then he asked if his son could work for them. Yes, he was told, as long as he did his work satisfactorily.

Then the two visited the plant, emptied of its seven or eight employees, who were out to lunch. The colonel's son Dick was there, however. Back went Mr. Owens and the colonel to the Brown Palace. By six they had a handshake. "My shake is a deal," said the colonel, but the lawyers also had to meet and the papers had to be signed nonetheless.

Continental's salesman in Denver at this time was Frank Hoffmann. Among his achievements had been to sell the first Continental coffee to go airborne, to Continental Airlines, which was based in Denver. He brewed coffee in the airline board room as a demonstration. When Robert Six, Continental Airline's chairman, asked whose coffee it was and was told Continental, he asked again, thinking he'd been misunderstood.

Denver salesman Frank Hoffmann in the late 1950s with a representative of Continental Airlines, the first carrier to take Continental coffee aloft.

When Mr. Hoffmann went to Los Angeles in 1960 to begin his West Coast career, Ben Kristopeit took over the Denver operation, which by now included the Spray roasting plant. Mr. Kristopeit, a tall, thin man, spoke the language of the chefs to whom he sold coffee and with whom he had rapport. A hard-hitting salesman, he came to Denver from Iowa, where he had been district sales manager.

In 1971, at Mr. Kristopeit's urging, Continental bought Western Paper Company, a Denver paper goods plant. This venture presented some special challenges, not all of which were overcome. The products were of such bulk that Continental drivers could not carry them in their panel trucks. Neither was the Continental warehouse big enough for this merchandise, and thus there could be no consolidation of the two operations. Moreover, Western's salesmen, mostly older men, found it a burden to adjust to the new owner. Some, in fact, retired when Continental took over.

Mr. Kristopeit meanwhile found himself using two warehouses and two distribution systems — Spray's and Western Paper's. It was not the most efficient way to operate. In any event, Denver roasting was discontinued not long afterwards, when Continental moved all its roasting to Houston. Continental sold its Denver buildings and combined its coffee and paper warehousing in a larger, rented warehouse.

Meanwhile, Continental moved in 1962 into coffee roasting in two other markets — San Antonio and St. Paul. The San Antonio acquisition was the Hoffman-Hayman Coffee Company, owned by the Menger family. This company, also called H&H, was founded in 1904 by W. R. Hoffman, who sold coffee door to door when the city had only 54,000 people, seventy-five grocers and a dozen or so restaurants. H&H was regarded in 1962 as one of the leading coffee firms in the Southwest. Gus Menger was chairman of the board, and his son Albert was president.

Stan Owens was vacationing with his family in Los Angeles when Jacob Cohn called and asked him to stop in San Antonio on his way back to discuss the purchase. Mr. Owens remembers the day, July 2, 1962, as blazing hot and oppressively humid. He cabbed it from the airport to the Menger Hotel (no relation to the coffee man). Next morning at 7:30, he and Albert Menger conferred in the hotel's coffee shop for a few hours and then visited the plant, where Mr. Owens met Gus Menger, the father. All three repaired to the Menger home for lunch. There they were joined by the Mengers' attorney, who had contacted Continental by letter suggesting the sale. Continental bought the company.

The other 1962 acquisition was the Eibert Coffee Company, of St. Paul. The Eibert name was well known in coffee circles. Lawrence J. Eibert, founder of the company in 1921, a promoter of the "fresh coffee" movement, had carried with him a pound of green coffee to draw attention to the cause. In his business he delivered coffee the day after he roasted it. His sons John and Paul, vice-president and vice-president-general manager respectively, had helped build the company.

Lawrence Eibert and Mr. Owens met in a hotel and were joined after a time by Lawrence's son Paul. The father left after lunch, leaving the other two to discuss matters further. Mr. Owens returned to Chicago that night, still not having seen the plant. A few days later, they agreed by telephone on a price.

Back Mr. Owens went to St. Paul, where he was finally given a tour of the plant. The apparent hesitancy to show him the plant was not unusual among coffee people, who are often secretive about their operations, in the view of industry veterans.

Robert Cohn also speaks of the "mystique" of coffee roasting, at least in decades past. There was a formula of sorts, a recipe for perfection that each roasting operation claimed for itself and was loath to reveal to people outside the operation. There was also the problem of spooking employees by showing a potential buyer around the place. So buyers were shown around either when no one else was there, as in Denver, or when the sale was a certainty.

Continental played to Eibert's strength with this purchase. Its own sales success in the area was modest, but Eibert's was substantial. So the Eibert name was kept while its business was being merged into Continental's — and that with the loss of only a few customers.

By the end of 1962, there were eight roasting plants — Chicago, Brooklyn, Toledo, Seattle, Denver, Glendale (Calif.), San Antonio and St. Paul. There was a difference in these post-Seattle acquisitions, namely the merging of Continental routes with those of the acquired companies. The pattern was to repeat itself time and again in succeeding decades, especially in the '70s, when a different kind of expansion took place that dwarfed this coffee expansion of the '50s and '60s.

The Twin Cities operation was later called Eibert Continental and finally just Continental. Meanwhile, Paul Eibert impressed Stan Owens with his abilities and let him know he'd like to grow with Continental, in or out of St. Paul. When an opening occurred in Chicago, therefore, Mr. Eibert was tapped for it. He took over Continental's personnel department.

Later he was put in charge of acquisitions. An acquisition once himself, he was able to tell sellers from experience what it was like to join the Continental family. His brother John became a vice-president-sales for Continental in St. Paul.

In 1963 Continental made a purchase in California which the company newsletter, "What's Brewin'?" said made it "a real power on the West Coast." This was the acquisition of the institutional foods division of J. A. Folger & Company — the same Folger who had blown Thomas Webb out of the water a few years earlier with its free mountain-grown coffee in the retail market. Continental already had a roasting plant in Vernon, near Los Angeles. With Folger came Jack L. Moore, who had started the division for Folger and then headed it for Continental.

In 1965 Continental came close to buying the Continental Coffee Company of Florida, in Miami, headed by Morry Koven. Mr. Koven had opened up Miami as a Continental sales manager in the 1930s and then had operated as a sort of Continental franchise for several decades.

Mr. Cohn was having dinner with Mr. Koven in Miami and suggested that Mr. Koven might want to merge with Continental. They agreed on the price with a handshake. Next day Mr. Cohn called Stan Owens, told him about the deal and asked him to have someone come down and take inventory the following week.

Mr. Owens knew Harry Davis was in Florida on vacation

and arranged with Mr. Davis to take the inventory. Several days before inventory time, Mr. Cohn visited the Florida plant. As he entered the shipping department, he saw a salesman walk out with two packages of coffee. A second salesman came in, picked up another package and left.

"Don't these men have to have invoices?" Mr. Cohn asked Mr. Koven.

"I know and trust these men," Mr. Koven answered.

"We don't run Continental that way," Mr. Cohn said. "If we buy your company, these men will not be able to get coffee without an invoice. We will have controls. Let me know tomorrow if you still want to sell."

Mr. Koven decided not to sell.

Five years later — two years after Mr. Cohn's death — Continental bought the Koven operation with the understanding that Continental controls would be in effect.

Up to 1965 the company bought fourteen companies, most of which have been discussed. They represented the company's coffee expansion to the nation. Purchases from 1967 to 1985 totalled seventy-five companies in a much different sort of expansion. But this coffee expansion made of Continental a national company.

The coffee expansion, unlike later full-line expansion, was not the result of any careful strategy. The purchases came entirely from contacts initiated by the sellers. Meanwhile, Continental entered other kinds of coffee markets. Chief among these was coffee-vending.

Vending had been growing since after World War II. Coffee, a high-markup item for the new industry, was a major part of it. The employee coffee break apparently invented by Jacob Cohn had spread and perhaps deteriorated by means of machines.

It had deteriorated in that coffee was no longer served by a woman pushing a cart past desks and offering free coffee with sugar and cream. Another form of deterioration was the vending machine's use of instant coffee. Continental was not about to sell coffee that didn't taste good, and instant was seen not to fill the bill.

But important Continental customers — ARA (for Automatic Retailers), Canteen, Servomation and others — had vending operations. So by the early 1950s, when the possibility arose of serving fresh-brew coffee in vending machines, Alvin Cohn as vice-president-sales made the key decision to put Continental's laboratory to work researching the matter.

Two researchers were put to work on the problem under direction of Dr. Jack Bloom. Within the industry Chicago was a hotbed of enthusiasm for fresh-brew vending, but technical difficulties abounded. At the heart of these difficulties was the dizzying variety of vending machines — thirteen in all, each brewing coffee at a different rate, ranging from a minute and a half to three minutes. This was the early "batch-brew" coffee, which brewed eight cups at a time which then might remain unused for a while before being drunk. Batch-brew vending machines were replaced by single-cup vendors which brewed coffee in the amazing time of six to eight seconds.

By September of 1956, Continental had set up its vending machine division under salesman Roy Zola for the vending of fresh-brewed coffee. Mr. Zola was a man at one time of over 300 pounds, an immaculate dresser with a hearty laugh and a warm smile.

This fresh-brew vended coffee had "restaurant-flavor," Continental claimed. The months of research and testing had led to the discovery of how to adjust blends and grinds to achieve the desired effect. The goal was reached. Fresh-brew vended coffee had arrived.

By May of 1960, "What's Brewin'?" was speaking of the "vast new market" developed with fresh brew in vending machines. Over the next year or so, every district sales manager was to come to Chicago to learn more about fresh-brew machines, no more than five of them at a time.

Two blends were being produced — rich and mild — for every major fresh-brew machine then being made. Each machine was unique; so the grind had to be adjusted for each. Company leaders had faced another question, whether to remain suppliers or to become vendors themselves. They decided to remain suppliers.

There had also been consideration of taking on the instant coffee challenge as well. The company went as far as installing bays for a spray drier when it moved into the Clybourn building in 1957. But no driers were installed. The Cohn brothers also gave thought to building an instant coffee plant but decided against it. They left themselves the option of building one offshore near a coffee-producing country but never acted on it.

Alvin Cohn pushed successfully for setting up an office coffee-service operation which prepared kits for office use. Again, the company decided to remain a supplier rather than a direct seller. Marketing executive Paul Friedman was put in charge of this operation, located in the Schubert Street plant in Chicago.

Hot chocolate sold well from vending machines in the '60s, rising a year after its introduction to near the top among Continental food items. At one point it was second only to salad dressings, a longtime staple of the Continental food line. For that matter, so was chocolate a longstanding item for Continental. At least since the '20s, dry chocolate mix was part of the Continental salesman's stock in trade.

Tea and four kinds of soup — chicken, beef, tomato, split pea — and a new non-dairy cream product were also Continental vending-machine items. Vending sales by 1964 were more than twenty percent of the company's total sales, and this at a time when Continental was the leading supplier of coffee to U. S. restaurants and hotels.

Indeed, among Continental field people in July of 1966 was vending specialist Sam Beckerman, whose job was "not to sell coffee," said "What's Brewin'?" but to keep customers informed about product innovations.

An important part of company effectiveness over these years of coffee expansion, as throughout its later history, was the Continental Employees Retirement Income Plan (CERIP) — a profit-sharing plan started in 1943.

The idea began with Jacob Cohn's worrying about his route salesmen, men who contributed so much to the company's success. At fifty or so, many of them were burnt out, because the work was so strenuous. Their work was physically demanding, not just because of the lifting and carrying of heavy loads but also because the men spent their days entering and leaving warm buildings in cold weather and cool ones in hot.

Mr. Cohn did not want to face a man who could no longer do the work after years of loyal service and have no more to offer him than a bit of severance pay. But if at that age they received only severance pay on leaving the company, it would not be fair, he reasoned.

Searching for a solution, he hit upon profit sharing, an arrangement that would permit salesmen to leave in their fifties with enough money in hand to start a restaurant or some other venture. Indeed, many route salesmen did go into the restaurant business.

Then he asked Stan Owens, his general manager, to meet with Henry Koven, the company's attorney, and Philip Rootberg, its accountant, and with them develop such a plan — not just for salesmen but for all employees. The three reviewed other companies' retirement plans but to their surprise found only a few profit sharing plans, and most of these were not attractive.

Only two had merit in their view — those of Sears, Roebuck and Joslyn Manufacturing Company. The spadework done, Messrs. Rootberg and Koven went ahead and developed a plan that in Stan Owens's opinion was ahead of its time. Their plan made employees eligible for 40% participation after only one year of employment, 100% after three years. Full vesting also came after three years, as opposed to ten years in most retirement plans. Contributions were entirely by the company.

The fund was started in 1943 with a $30,000 company contribution. In two years it had 160 participants. By 1960 the company contribution for the year had risen to $450,000, with 610 participants. The fund's value had risen to almost $3 million. The fund had more than doubled every five years since 1945. Nothing of it came from pay checks; all was from company profits. Between 1958 and 1961, this company contribution came to 13.8% of participating employees' earnings. The company newsletter pointed out that this was comparable to receiving an extra month's wages.

By July of 1961 the average profit sharing account had $4,575, all invested in high-grade stocks and bonds. More than $700,000 had been paid to participants who had retired or resigned. Each employee received a bankbook-like yearly statement from Continental Bank, the fund's corporate trustee, which gave the balance at the end of the previous year, the amount contributed by the company and earnings applied to the employee's account in the year just ended, and the year-end total. Every employee thus knew exactly what he had in the fund at the end of every year.

Labor relations were another important aspect of company life. Stanley Owens as general manager was asked by Jacob Cohn to sit in on a contract negotiation in the early 1940s with the driver-salesmen's union. Negotiations were done at the time by a committee consisting of the owners of three good-sized coffee companies who negotiated for the Green Coffee Association. This committee negotiated an industry-wide contract in Chicago.

Once this negotiation was completed, Mr. Cohn asked Mr. Owens to represent Continental in future negotiations, both with the driver-salesmen, members of the International Brotherhood of Teamsters, and with the urn-manufacturing employees, members of the United Sheet Metal Workers. It was very difficult, he said, for an owner to negotiate with unions who as a matter of course told him as an owner how he should run his business.

Early in 1944 the Congress of Industrial Organizations (CIO) tried to organize Continental's packing and shipping people. An election was held, and the employees voted not to join the union. They already had hospitalization insurance and profit-sharing. The CIO had little to offer them.

Six months later a man called Stan Owens from Teamsters Local 738, not the one to which the drivers belonged, intent on organizing these same packing and shipping people and asking for a meeting. "We just beat the CIO, and I see no point in meeting with the Teamsters," Mr. Owens told the man.

"I know," he replied. "And they'll try again, but we want you for the Teamsters before they do. Before you say you're not going to meet with me, call your lawyer. Then call me back."

Mr. Owens called Henry Koven, who explained that by law Continental had to meet with the Teamsters representative. They set up a luncheon meeting — Messrs. Cohn, Owens and Koven and the union man. It started friendly enough, but then the Teamsters representative explained his intentions, namely to sign the employees without an election and to picket Continental if he were not allowed to do it.

Mr. Cohn, confused, turned to Henry Koven and asked, "Does this mean I have to force my employees to join the union even if they do not want to?" Mr. Koven said they should discuss that later.

"If you don't agree to this," continued the union man, "we will picket your plant, and there will be no trucks going in or out twenty-four hours a day. You have a railroad track in back of your plant. We know how to handle that." He and his associates would handle it as they had handled a similar situation when Chicago Mail Order Company used its railroad spur to circumvent a picketing. On this occasion six employees of the local lay on the tracks and blocked the train, forcing Chicago Mail Order to give in.

Jacob Cohn was dismayed by the union's approach. He was willing to accept unionization of the shippers and handlers if he lost an election, but he was not willing to hand his employees over to a union without their approval.

But the union was within its rights under current labor law, Mr. Koven explained later. It was sign with this local or be picketed. Mr. Cohn agreed reluctantly but left the signing of the contract to Mr. Owens. Not only was Mr. Cohn unhappy with the arrangement, but several employees came to him to ask why it was happening. The unionized workers under this local received only a nickel an hour raise the first year and no raise at all the second.

In Toledo from 1948 on, a different situation presented itself. The coffee employees had somehow become members of the brewery workers union, based in South Bend, Indiana. Breweries' profit margins were much greater than food companies', and brewery workers' wages were higher as a result. This made it difficult in negotiations to keep the Toledo employees' wages in line with the foodworkers' scale, which was lower.

Mr. Owens, by now the regular contract negotiator for the company and liking the challenge, regularly had the Continental branch manager sit in on negotiations. In Toledo this was Leonard Giunto, in New York Simon Rice, etc. He also brought Lou Leichentritt into many negotiations, to give Mr. Leichentritt experience and to provide backup for himself.

The Toledo wage-scale situation was a problem for the first negotiator Mr. Owens and Mr. Giunto dealt with, who apparently could not understand why coffee workers could not be paid as well as brewery workers. He was succeeded after a year by Mel Greenthal, a more knowledgeable man, who understood the situation.

In California as in Chicago, meanwhile, Mr. Owens became spokesman for area coffee companies, which included companies at the time much bigger than Continental.

Through thirty-five years of contract negotiations beginning in the early 1940s, Continental did not have a strike. Labor-union relations were characterized, says Stan Owens, by "mutual respect, understanding and cooperation." But at the start of that period, the company suffered from somebody else's strike, namely the over-the-road truck drivers.

This 1944 national strike threatened Continental, which in the late 1930s had switched from trains to trucks as its means of moving coffee from city to city. Train service had proven undependable. The 1944 strike hit at Continental's ability to move coffee and food products to its markets outside Chicago and Brooklyn.

On the day the strike was called, Mr. Cohn walked over to Stan Owens's office and said very quietly: "You know we must get merchandise to our salesmen. Do anything you feel is necessary, but get the merchandise to the men." Then he walked out of the building to call on customers.

Mr. Owens contacted Howard Mortimer, the plant superintendent, who was responsible for order filling and shipping. He said one solution was to use Railway Express, which was expensive but fast.

But Continental rarely used Railway Express; and when Mr. Mortimer called, he was told no trucks were available. The strike affected over-the-road, or highway trucking between cities; trucks within cities were free to operate. Neither were the railroads on strike; so the goal was to move the merchandise to the trains.

Then Mr. Owens called Railway Express and got the area supervisor, whom he persuaded to sit down and talk about it at Continental. The supervisor had the same story: no trucks.

But Mr. Owens managed to persuade the man, and by noon of that first day of the strike, Railway Express had five trucks waiting at Continental's loading dock.

But the Railway Express trucks could handle only a small part of what had to be shipped, and Mr. Owens decided to rent trucks to haul merchandise to the New York Central Railroad docks near Michigan Avenue and South Water Street.

Three big Hertz trucks were rented, brought to the Continental plant at 375 West Ontario Street, loaded and driven to the railroad docks. It went this way for two days, until rail shipments were embargoed. A new strategy was needed.

It was decided to drive rented trucks inter-city, loaded mainly with coffee, since there wouldn't be room for both coffee and allied products. One went off to Toledo, another to Iowa, a third to Lansing, Michigan, a fourth to Wisconsin — each to route salesmen in their territories.

Detroit presented a special problem. Reports had come back of strike-connected violence there. Mr. Owens called Al Marans, the Detroit district sales manager, and asked him to have his five route men drive to Chicago in their half-ton panel delivery trucks. They would arrive in Chicago on a Saturday night, load up and be off for Detroit Sunday morning. They would not be bothered on the way, because theirs were smaller trucks than those used for over-the-road hauling.

The men arrived at the plant Saturday night and drove into the garage, where their trucks were loaded. They spent the night at the St. Clair Hotel and left early the next morning for Detroit, carrying mostly coffee, and enough of that for several days' deliveries.

Meanwhile, the big rented trucks continued the Toledo, Iowa, etc. runs for several more days, until finally the Army was sent in to take over the trucks and inter-city service was restored. The strike was over, and none too soon. Another week of it, and Continental Coffee Company would have been hurt, especially because of the dent it put in allied-products sales.

Nonetheless, the over-the-road truckers' strike of 1944 is remembered as the time when coffee, like the mail, got through no matter the obstacles.

On another front completely, there is the matter of a corporate philosophy. Sometime early in the '60s, Robert Cohn started Continental on its way to developing such a philosophy. It was probably one of the first companies to develop one.

"We encourage vertical and horizontal communication throughout all parts of our organization," the Continental philosophy says.

Furthermore, it encourages activism in Continental employees. Continental, the corporate philosophy reads, "acknowledges and accepts its responsibilities to our society . . . Our people and our company should take active roles within our society, going beyond responsiveness alone."

In that vein, the company offers "encouragement and assistance to those who wish to participate in charitable, civic or political activities of their choice."

This participation has taken various forms, from helping raise money for civic and charitable groups to more visible tasks requiring greater public commitment, such as Alvin Cohn's involvement in Junior Achievement in Chicago.

Mr. Cohn has been Chicago-area president of this organization, which aims at encouraging young people in business and the professions. He also has been an aggressive and effective fund-raiser for such organizations as the Jewish United Fund and served for more than ten years on the board of Michael Reese Hospital.

Robert also has been a generous contributor to the Fund and other charitable enterprises, aware as his father was that with economic success came responsibility that went beyond "responsiveness alone." He has served on the board of the National College of Education, in Evanston, and has headed a Chicago organization formed to help and encourage minority businessmen.

Another who took the corporate philosophy seriously was Stanley Owens, who during the '60s and '70s headed up the Citizens Schools Committee in Chicago. In this capacity he was recommended several times to Mayor Richard J. Daley for appointment to the Chicago Board of Education. Mayor Daley never appointed him, but when he named an advisory commission on school board nominations, Mr. Owens was among its members. He eventually chaired this commission and on one occasion received a private mayoral tongue-lashing when he publicly opposed the mayor.

The occasion was Mr. Owens's public comments about the mayor's motives in bypassing his own advisory commission when he reappointed a school board president, John D. Carey. "He's just trying to prove Mike Royko [author of the recently published highly critical book about Daley, *Boss*] is right," Mr. Owens told a reporter, and the mayor bawled him out over the telephone the next day.

After the advisory commission approved the Carey reappointment after the fact, Mr. Owens termed "hogwash" the mayor's claim that he was not required to seek the commission's approval for the reappointment. "The members of the commission couldn't figure out why Daley acted as he did unless he just wanted to show us who runs the school board," Mr. Owens told the *Chicago Tribune*.

But the matter blew over, and later the mayor invited Mr. Owens to come and see him, and their meeting was a friendly one. Mr. Owens headed the advisory commission for ten years until it was abolished peremptorily by Mayor Jane Byrne in 1979.

Continental's coffee expansion to the nation is a story of acquisition of companies — fourteen in all up to 1965 — and of the development of a company from regional to national.

Jacob Cohn died on June 28, 1968, of a heart attack. He

had done his work well. His sons were there to carry it on. It is time, before we close this section devoted to coffee expansion to the nation, to look at the man Jacob Cohn as colleagues and family remember him.

Jacob Cohn, his sons and Stanley Owens at the Jacob Cohn home in 1965 for a private celebration of Continental's first fifty years. *From left:* Robert Cohn, Jacob Cohn, Alvin Cohn and Stanley Owens.

9. JACOB COHN THE MAN

Jacob Cohn's monument is the company he started in 1915. Above all, therefore, his leadership qualities command consideration.

Joe Davis, one of his early employees and one of his most resourceful salesmen, "listened and followed with blind faith" when Mr. Cohn spoke, such was his confidence in the man. "If I were you . . ." Mr. Cohn would begin, and Mr. Davis would take what he said "as a command."

Mr. Cohn asked him if he had a tuxedo, and Mr. Davis, then a shipping room employee, went out and bought one for $8 on Maxwell Street, Chicago's open-air market on the West Side. A few days later Mr. Cohn took him as his guest to a restaurant association formal dinner, dressed in his new tux.

Mr. Davis bought his first stock in the company when he was eighteen years old, on Mr. Cohn's suggestion he do so. A small-town boy from Iowa, he knew nothing about stocks, but Mr. Cohn was for him "the example of the perfect life," and his suggestion was enough.

Mr. Cohn inspired people to do what they didn't think they could do, recalled Louis Leichentritt, a longtime employee and Continental executive. He gave strength to others to stay on when the going got tough, says Aaron Clark, a longtime financial advisor. He was like a coach who "crystallized" others' efforts to produce a winning combination, said another man who worked briefly for the company just before World War II and later put in a lifetime in the foodservice industry though not with Continental.

He listened, communicated his optimism, was able to retain a great deal of information and was uncompromising in pursuit of company goals. When his son Alvin, then a very young route salesman, brought in a returned case of salad dressing, Mr. Cohn told him to go back out and sell it to another customer.

When a salesman in Iowa answered the phone once too often early in the day when he should have been out on the road selling, he was fired. When the sales manager solved a problem, he congratulated the man and promptly urged him to go out and solve some more. Mr. Cohn was not long on praise for doing what his employees were supposed to do.

He was practical and pragmatic. He told his bride-to-be Belle, who was also to be the mother of his three sons, that they would have to live on $50 a week or put off getting married. The rest would go to build the business.

He made his son Alvin president of the company when Alvin was only thirty-seven, so that he could learn while he was relatively young whether he could do the job.

He was himself a master salesman and had already done anything he expected his salesmen to do. His business principles included not accepting a lunch or dinner from a supplier, to whom he would then feel indebted. He told his buyers to take the same approach.

Spotting trouble in the plant, he acted immediately, calling the needed help personally, as in the case of the repair man at the Ontario Street plant, when two coffee packaging machines were down for fifteen minutes. He had noticed the problem while walking through the plant. His advice to Stan Owens as his general manager was to walk through the plant twice a day, once each in morning and afternoon.

When his chief urn-maker blew up at Stan Owens, who had

Jacob Cohn receives from Stanley Owens a tribute from employees at Continental's fiftieth-anniversary celebration in 1965.

passed on to him a customer's complaint, rushing down two flights of stairs to confront Mr. Owens personally, Mr. Cohn accepted the veteran's resignation on the spot. The urn-maker declared he would not take it any more from "young punks."

"He has to learn how to act," Mr. Cohn told Mr. Owens. A week later, the man returned repentant. Mr. Cohn delivered the man's apology to Mr. Owens. He admitted he was "excitable," though more as excuse than confession, and Mr. Cohn asked "Are you going to change?" He didn't, however, and continued to vent irritation on his underlings. He later left the company.

With all his firmness, Mr. Cohn was ready to help people in ways that went beyond strict business requirements. A restaurant owner who had not been a customer during the prosperous 1920s turned to Mr. Cohn for credit in the 1930s, when others refused it. Mr. Cohn extended credit to the man, who was unable to pay. Later he showed up at Mr. Cohn's office looking for a sales job, a big, hulking fellow once successful but now with sharply diminished prospects.

Mr. Cohn instructed Mr. Owens to hire him. Mr. Owens sent him out with samples. He made just two sales in three months. Feeling sorry for the man, Mr. Cohn told Mr. Owens to keep him on for two more months and then let him go.

In various ways he showed himself sensitive to employees. He bawled one out for working too late. Another, a young man newly hired in Pittsburgh, happened to be present at the time of the firm's annual meeting, and he invited him to sit in on it — something the man never forgot in years of working for Continental.

He would investigate a suggestion by anyone, even if it seemed absurd. He would have Stan Owens check it out and then act on Mr. Owens's recommendation. He didn't want to get into the habit of ignoring people's ideas, especially employees'.

His willingness to try things showed itself when he bought Brazilian-government (DNC) green coffee which others shied away from. Mr. Cohn tested it, then ordered a small shipment, then progressively bigger shipments. Once satisfied it was of good quality, he bought much larger quantities well before other coffee buyers realized the value involved, saving a lot of money in the process.

He didn't want to be fooled, but he was fair. He heard a district sales manager was starting late and working at his own business on the side. He put a Pinkerton detective on the man for four days, found he was doing fine, and tore up the Pinkerton's report.

He had taken it on the chin from his office manager in the company's early days, then years later dealt with him firmly but without rancor. This man walked off on a Saturday with the "customer cards," each with a customer's address and the blend, package size and quantity of coffee he used.

The cards were at the heart of order-filling. Without them the system was disrupted. The man knew what he would do with the cards. He had hired his own salesmen who on Monday made the rounds of Continental customers falsely informing them that Continental was going out of business. If the customers wanted coffee, these salesmen said, they should order from this new company.

Meanwhile, Continental employees arrived on Monday to find trouble. They could neither write orders nor ship goods without the cards. Not until Monday night, when Continental salesmen returned with most of the information on the stolen cards were they ready to return to normal procedures.

The manager's plan worked moderately well. He got a foothold in the business and did fairly well in it for a number of years. Then some thirty years later, he offered to sell his business to Mr. Cohn. Mr. Cohn thanked him but said he wasn't interested.

Jacob Cohn shrank from business decisions that hurt others. In 1950 he was on the verge of buying a Brooklyn coffee company whose plant was much bigger than Continental's Brooklyn plant. Lou Leichentritt and Stan Owens had been working on the deal for a month. An agreement had been reached, and lawyers were drawing up documents.

Then Mr. Cohn went to see the place. Walking through, he saw a number of employees in their fifties and sixties. Many of these, according to the logic of the deal, he would have to lay off, since a merging of the two facilities would be in order. He decided to call off the acquisition. He did not want to be the one to lay off these older workers, who would have special trouble finding new jobs.

Earlier, in the 1930s some longtime customers were in trouble and he was being forced to deny them credit. Rather

Jacob Cohn with some Continental stalwarts in the early '50s. *Standing, from left:* Dan Pacini, Robert Campbell, Jacob Cohn, Bernard Pippenger, Aaron A. Good, Roy Zola. *Front, from left:* Stanley Owens and Dr. Jack Bloom.

than be the one to give the bad news, he left the country on a coffee buying trip to South America, as if fleeing the hard situation that was beyond his ability to correct.

When he could do something about a problem, he did. Route salesmen, as we have seen, faced a burn-out problem as they got older. Mr. Cohn established a profit-sharing plan. The company ran into a snag when its banker at First National Bank of Chicago demonstrated feeble interest in setting it up for them. Instead he advised Mr. Owens to call him six months later.

"Mr. Owens," said Mr. Cohn after a moment's surprise when he heard about it, "hasn't Mr. Powell from Continental Bank been calling on us for our business?" A call to Mr. Powell got immediate results. Continental Bank set up the profit-sharing account and in the process began a permanent full-scale relationship with Continental Coffee Company.

In business situations Jacob Cohn was always "Mister

Cohn," and with one or two exceptions he addressed others as "Mister" also. It was as much a part of his style as his wrinkle-free face. Stanley Owens worked at his right hand for twenty-eight years, and apart from social situations, as on the golf course, he was always "Mister Owens."

The habit bespoke Jacob Cohn's sense of dignity, his dignified manner, and his alertness to others' sensibilities. Calling on a Chinese restaurateur in the Loop, he regularly addressed him as "Mister." The man finally took him aside and told him he was the only salesman who did so. The rest called him "Charley," which was not his name. And with that he gave Mr. Cohn his business.

Many years later Mr. Cohn overheard a young summer employee calling his superiors by their first names, as the young man had been told to do. He called in the two older men and asked them who this young man was and why he was on a first-name basis with his superiors.

He encouraged ambition, especially among salesmen. When a district sales manager earned more than he did, he was not only not bothered by that, he was delighted. It was his greatest pleasure to see the company prosper and its employees with it.

On the other hand, he urged discretion on a sales manager who drove a Cadillac, counseling him not to park it in front of a customer's or prospect's place of business while making calls. "They will think there's too much profit in the coffee business and it might hurt our company," he said.

Personally, he was not motivated by money. He wanted Continental to provide the best coffee and the best service, and he wanted it to grow. He tried to motivate salesmen with suggestions of good things that awaited their success — a bigger house, education for their children, pleasant vacations and the like.

He measured success in goods and services delivered, "tonnage" not just profits. He drove his own car until his sons, concerned about his distracted driving habits, persuaded him to get a chauffeur. Years later he reasserted himself and returned to driving his own car.

Jacob Cohn was a man of principle but not a forbidding man. He was firm but fair and had a sense of humor. "Not the easiest guy to work with," said one who worked closely with him over two decades. "He could read you in a minute. When he asked you a question, he wanted an answer." Others said the same thing. Everybody said Jacob Cohn was a fair man.

If you admitted your mistake, it was all right. If you lied to him, he would flush with anger, even "cut you to pieces," one man said. He never raised his voice, but that was small consolation to the employee who one day proudly announced a newly discovered money-saving device and was asked by Mr. Cohn, "Why didn't you think about this five years ago?"

He considered it self-defeating to carry a grudge. He hired back one of two brothers, cousins of his who had walked off the job to work for a competitor, leaving their salesmen's trucks in the field. When the man developed an illness that required his being dismissed, Mr. Cohn instructed Mr. Owens to keep him on the payroll, where he stayed until his death.

He might hire someone in trouble, but he wouldn't keep him if the person turned out a bad employee, because other employees' morale would be hurt in such a case. His advice to Stan Owens as a beginning manager was to hire the best he could find, even if they were better than he, and not to worry about protecting his own job.

Surround yourself with "twos and threes" and you will be second or third, he said. Surround yourself with "ones and twos" and you will be first or second. If you are not first or second, your ones and twos will leave you, he said.

He was unswerving in enforcing the company prohibition against buying business. The salesman who promised a new canopy to the customer in Cleveland was fired, but the customer got the canopy.

Mr. Cohn did not finish high school, but he took various self-improvement courses, as in public speaking and letter-writing. He came to this country when he was eight years old, late enough to give him an accent, but he worked to eradicate it, and no accent was discernible.

On the company's 50th anniversary in 1965, he was given a plaque at the annual company credit union dinner, paid for by employees at $1 each. When Stan Owens presented the award on their behalf, it was a surprise to him.

He was a family man, taking trips with his wife Belle and their three sons, Alvin, Robert and Stanley, and later with his second wife, Rosaline, whom he married after Belle died, and their daughter, Marcia.

He had "some tricks," as Gerald Ryan, his personal secretary for many years, recalls. He would always ask, "Why did you do that?"—even when the question seemed unwarranted. One day Mr. Ryan asked him in return, "Mr. Cohn, how would you have done it?" Mr. Cohn got red, then chuckled, and Mr. Ryan pressed his advantage. "Please don't do that," he asked his boss.

"I won't do it again," said Mr. Cohn.

Among the relationships Mr. Cohn was proudest of in the 1930s was his friendship with George Cardinal Mundelein, Chicago's Roman Catholic archbishop. The two traded invitations to fund-raising dinners of their respective faiths, Catholic and Jewish. Mr. Cohn was also close to Bishop Bernard Sheil of the Chicago archdiocese, founder of the Catholic Youth Organization. Mr. Cohn himself was on the board of a West Side orphanage.

From one of Mr. Cohn's many affiliations with charitable organizations in later life, he learned to respect an idea promoted and implemented by his sons. This was the notion of using a budget. Mr. Cohn didn't see the need for it at first.

His position was that you just did the best you could all the time. But after attending some meetings of the charity on whose board he served, where the budget was the main item of discussion, he began to see budgeting in a different light. The people on the board with him were people he knew and respected. He decided his sons and their colleagues had the right idea after all.

A decade or so earlier he had had doubts about another, more basic facet of the Continental organization, namely the number of employees at work in the Chicago office, which handled the sales accounts with their intricate system of controls.

A friend in heavy manufacturing, a different sort of business, questioned the employment of sixty or seventy people. Mr. Cohn asked Mr. Owens to discuss the matter with his friend. He did so, explaining how these employees each contributed to the complex, detailed process of keeping track of what was sold to whom for how much by whom, etc.

The man at length was convinced and withdrew his objection. Mr. Owens informed Mr. Cohn, who was satisfied on the matter and added this comment: "Pardon me," he said, in a typical opening. "I want you to run the place without too many but enough people."

Finally, there was the comment by Jacob Cohn to Mr. Owens when they attended the funeral of an industry figure. They arrived to find the funeral chapel full of flowers, contributed by mourners and the bereaved.

Viewing the floral display, Mr. Cohn in an aside to Mr. Owens made an observation that may stand as a sort of epitaph for him as well as advice to the rest of us. "Too bad he can't smell them," he said. "We should always give flowers to people when they can smell them."

PART THREE

Foodservice to the Nation

The Cohn brothers and Stanley Owens with 1981 winners of the Jacob Cohn scholarship awards. *From left:* Mr. Owens, Jillisa Brittan, Alvin Cohn, Teri Walker, Robert Cohn, Adam Caribi.

10. ALVIN AND ROBERT COHN: THE SALESMAN AND THE PLANNER

When Alvin Cohn was a small boy, he played on top of the 133-pound bags of green coffee at the Continental plant on Ontario Street. When he and his father passed restaurants on the street, he would ask, "Are we selling that place?" He grew up with coffee and coffee-selling in his blood.

In 1930 or 1931, he and his parents and two brothers and a cousin took a trip to Brazil. Alvin was ten years old. His father, beseiged by customers asking loans to tide themselves over the hard times, wanted some relief. He left his coffee company in the hands of his organization and went south.

With the family came Toby Katz, a cousin, who took care of Mrs. Cohn, already stricken with the illness that was to be fatal for her. It was Mr. Cohn's first trip to Brazil, where most of his coffee came from. While down there, he bought a coffee-maker which didn't work and some coffee which he sold in New York at a profit that paid for the trip.

In 1936 Alvin began work in summer in the packing department, running rush orders for Joe Katz, the city sales manager. The other Katz brother, Leon, was Continental's general manager.

That year, 1936, Alvin started high school, leaving the city to attend Culver Military Academy, in northern Indiana. The family lived at the time at 5500 West Congress Street, on Chicago's Far West Side. Among their neighbors were the Kovens. The father of this family was Henry Koven, an immigrant from England and Continental's lawyer. Young Howard Koven, later to succeed his father in that role, played ping-pong with the Cohn boys in the basement of their Congress Street home.

After a year at Culver, Alvin came back and spent the next two years at Austin High, the area's public school, working summers as a vacation-relief route salesman. He drove a panel truck and lugged cases of coffee and other products in the hot weather.

One summer he took over Henry Hirsch's route, in a neighborhood where cooking oil sold well. He'd return from a day's work spattered with oil from "leakers." He did not complain to his father, however. "You didn't," he said years later—even if your name was Cohn.

Alvin returned to Culver for his senior year, graduating in 1939. The next year, he began at DePaul University, more to please his father — an avid proponent of schooling, of which he himself had a limited amount — as much as anything else.

His father would drop him off at DePaul in the morning. In the afternoon he sold coffee, soliciting from a truck in a long, narrow strip from Lake Michigan to Mannheim Road (as far west as where O'Hare airport is today) and from North Avenue to Fullerton Avenue.

Mr. Cohn asked Stanley Owens, who joined the company about this time, if he would help Alvin with his school work. Mr. Owens did so but after a time had to tell the father what he may have known already, that the son's heart was not in schooling. "He can't wait to get into this business," Mr. Owens told him.

Alvin also wanted to get married. But in Chicago the situation was not promising for him. Joe Katz, a longtime employee, was city sales manager. In Brooklyn, New York, where the company's roasting plant and sales operation were losing money, it was another story. Mr. Cohn was going to sell the Brooklyn plant, but Alvin urged him not to and said he wanted to go there. Mr. Owens also urged Mr. Cohn to send Alvin to New York.

So a few weeks after Alvin was married on Thanksgiving Day, 1941, in Chicago, he and his bride arrived in New York after their Florida honeymoon, Alvin to be vice-president-sales at the Brooklyn branch. He had his disappointments, when wartime controls on coffee sales presented Continental with some tough choices — whether to take on new, big customers or remain loyal to old, smaller ones. Alvin lost some very big new accounts when his father chose to stay with the old customers.

"You have to say that my father was an unusual, honorable kind of guy," Alvin says. "When he gave you his word, that was it."

In another incident, Mr. Cohn took a call from a major restaurant owner who offered him twenty-five cents a pound over the legal limit for coffee. "Don't you ever call me again," said Mr. Cohn and hung up. Stan Owens recalls a similar offer of business from a state agency, with the requirement of a political kickback. This too was refused.

Back from the service after the war, Alvin went to work as a downtown route salesman under Chicago city sales manager Marvin Sommers. "If he makes it, he stays. If he doesn't, he goes," Jacob Cohn told Mr. Sommers. Six months later, Mr. Sommers happily reported that the young man was going to make it.

Alvin was succeeding though full of youthful frustration at what he considered his slow pace of advancement. He'd come back expecting to be a sales manager, but that wasn't quite his fathers' way of doing things. He quit twice but never convincingly enough to make it stick. When Mr. Sommers went to Milwaukee, Alvin took over as city sales manager.

It was the chance he'd been waiting for. He'd had his taste

of big selling in New York, and now he set his sights on the big Chicago-based accounts, including national chains.

He called on Joe Szabo, president of Szabo Food Service, an industrial caterer, and his executive vice-president Ray Longworth. He called on Bill Fishman, president of the recently established ARA Services, whom he had known before ARA was put together, and his buyer, Erwin Stup. Vending-machine operators were selling out to ARA right and left, including Sidney Rudin, a Continental customer of increasing importance; so it was self-defense to get the ARA business.

Others he contacted were Moe Glockner, buyer for Canteen Corporation, and Kemmons Wilson, founder-president of Holiday Inns. At Motorola, located at the time on Augusta Boulevard on the city's West Side, he took on the daunting task of convincing the man in charge of that company's cafeteria, Fred Hansen, that Continental was the coffee for him.

Some of these contacts were cold calls. All were developed by a combination of salesmanship and helpfulness that brought the customers in one by one. If he had to go out of his way to help, that's what he did. Fred Hansen, for instance, faced with the pleasurable duty of greeting Danish royalty when they visited Chicago, turned to Alvin for help in making arrangements.

He sold these big accounts and showed other Continental salesmen they could be sold. Some of these, outside Chicago, hearing of his successes with the chains, would ask him to come and accompany them on calls to these potential customers. Bernard Pippenger, the Indiana sales manager, for one, would ask Alvin to do this. So did Bob Campbell in Cincinnati.

This major sales work by Alvin began in the late '40s and extended into the '50s. Alvin did a fair amount of traveling at this time, visiting men in the field, holding sales meetings and beginning to acquire within and outside Continental a reputation as "Mister Continental."

One who remembers the role Alvin played in these years is Marvin Sommers, the former Chicago city sales manager, who in 1952 took over New York and East Coast sales. Alvin once sat until three in the morning one Christmas Day with Mr. Sommers when a situation developed that got him very discouraged. Mr. Sommers had been ready to quit, but Alvin talked him out of it and promised the problem would be solved.

Once Alvin had to bring a perplexing order from his father to the sales managers, to add a nickel a pound to the coffee price. His father had called him in and told him to do so. "Has the price of green coffee gone up?" he asked his father. No, it hadn't. "Then why are we raising our price?" Alvin asked. Just do it, his father said.

The sales managers weren't happy to hear the news, and indeed some minor problems resulted, mainly from the fact that their competitors had not raised their prices. After a few weeks, during which sales held up well enough, Jacob Cohn called Alvin in again, and told him to reduce the price a nickel.

Alvin was glad to hear this but had to ask his father, "Dad, why did you do this?"

"To test our sales force," Jacob Cohn said. "I wanted to see how good they are."

Whether passing on difficult orders from his father or consoling the discouraged, Alvin was a "moderating force" for salesmen, Mr. Sommers recalls. He inspired them at the same time. Sentimental and full of feeling, he would cry at the drop of the hat. Years later, at a goodbye dinner for Mr. Sommers, who was retiring, Alvin was on the verge of breaking down when Mr. Sommers told him, "Alvin, don't get maudlin," and the affair continued in good spirits. At the annual restaurant shows, "everybody came to him." He became "a legend in the industry," another longtime executive recalls.

Alvin drove when he had to, including his New York trips.

But in time flying seemed the way to go, and the company bought an Aerocommander airplane. A route salesman who was also a pilot flew it for a time, but he turned out a better route man than pilot. A full-time professional pilot, Dick Buckau, was hired, and Alvin began to have smoother flights. Later he traded the Aerocommander in for a DC-3. It was a far cry from his father selling coffee from a horsedrawn wagon.

Alvin operated in a sense without portfolio. Another man, Walter Belinky, had the sales manager title. Not until 1958, when his father made him president, did he have a title commensurate with the role he had undertaken. He was thirty-seven years old.

If Alvin Cohn was Mister Outside, like Glenn Davis for the postwar Army football teams, ever the salesman and contact man, his brother Robert was Mister Inside, like Davis's teammate Felix Blanchard, ever the planner and systematic thinker who plotted Continental's future.

Robert Cohn, five years younger than Alvin, has his boyhood recollections of Continental Coffee Company too. He recalls coffee packages ready for shipment from Ontario Street with customers' names handwritten on them — a personal touch difficult to imagine in our day. While in high school he worked summers wrapping packages to order.

The rush order department where he worked, on the first floor, used a "sedan delivery" to handle emergency calls — a pound of pepper, five pounds of coffee, and the like. On the fourth floor was food manufacturing, where Jack Bloom held forth. Bob Cohn once spent a day filling Worcestershire sauce bottles by hand. The smell got to him, and he became sick.

Another thing he recalls is how at the end of the day the cashier brought the bank balance, on adding-machine tapes, to Jacob Cohn, his father. Mr. Cohn always wanted to know the cash balance, even when the company had a lot of business and it was not a problem, as it had been in earlier days.

He also remembers Louie Nardella, most of his teeth missing, working hard at his tough job of lugging 133-pound bags of green coffee all day. On hot days, a fan was set up to blow over a bushel of ice. Chaff from the roasting machine blew in through the screened windows. Even on the hottest days, Jacob Cohn always wore a tie, shirt and jacket.

Mr. Cohn was a severe critic of his own coffee and got "very upset" if it did not taste good, Robert recalls. On the other hand, he felt very good if it came out right.

In those days Robert Cohn remembers "a certain mystique" attached to the roasting of coffee. The Jabez Burns Company was considered the only roaster manufacturer worth thinking about. The Jabez Burns installation engineer, Ken Burns, a bald, heavy-set man who rarely spoke, was the only one who knew how the equipment worked, as far as Continental was concerned.

The aroma of roasted coffee permeated the neighborhood in those days before environmental controls, much like the bygone smell of burning leaves. It was a pleasant smell to which no one objected. The chaff from roasted beans that flew out of the roaster was another matter. It lay like dust on flat surfaces and in warm weather blew through open windows on to office workers' desks.

Robert Cohn finished high school in the early '40s, served in the Merchant Marine during the war, and graduated from Northwestern University in 1947. A week after graduation, he was delivering coffee on route B, from Lawrence Avenue in the city to north suburban Waukegan. A college friend saw him delivering coffee and asked him why he was doing this type of work, thinking that Bob Cohn had come on hard times and couldn't get better work than driving a truck.

That fall he made regular trips back to the Northwestern campus to deliver and brew coffee for the university president and his guests under Dyche Stadium on home-game football Saturdays. In this way he got perhaps closer to the president as a coffee salesman than he ever did as a student.

On the route his "bible" was the route book — seventy-five to eighty cards in a leather holder, each bearing a customer's name and the history of his purchases. Invoices were kept in a kind of pocket behind the cards. Back at the plant, truck loaders followed the invoices' sequence as they filled the orders, thus loading the trucks in the order of delivery.

He recalls the Saturday-morning sales meetings to which samples of Continental and competitors' coffee were brought, brewed and submitted to blind-testing by Continental salesmen. Continental coffee won nine out of ten times.

He remembers too when Continental went for the Hilton Hotels' business in the early '50s and would have gotten it if it had national distribution. This was before fresh-packing techniques. Coffee had a short shelf life and transportation was not what it is today. But Continental had only three plants, none west of Chicago.

Bob Cohn ran route B for a year or so, working for part of this time on green coffee with Bill Meyer, the buyer. Then one day, while he and his father were driving home from Ontario Street, his father asked him if he would leave in the morning for Toledo, where Continental had just bought a new coffee company. He said he would. It was 1948.

Bob spent nine months or so in Toledo heading up the newly acquired Karavan Coffee operation, where truck shipments of food products arrived twice a week from Chicago. Continental made wide use of premiums in those days. offering glasses or jars for big orders of gelatin or tea and the like. Decisions to use or not use premiums seemed "hit or miss" to Bob Cohn, who already, at the ripe age of twenty-three, was seeking more rational, systematic ways of doing things.

Indeed, intuition seemed to decide everything. Roasting was decided by color, for instance. The roaster would say coffee was "a shade too high." Bob Cohn would ask, "What's a shade?" "A shade is a shade," he would be told.

Or a grind was judged "too fine," and the roasters were

told to "coarsen it up a little." In contrast to such practices, Bob Cohn started grind analysis and put thermostats in the roaster as a quality-control mechanism. He was looking for ways to control the process. He wanted to make sense out of what he was doing.

In 1950 or so, his father sent him to Brazil. Why, he was not sure. Partly to learn the business, he assumed. His father was "not a big planner." Bob was twenty-four years old. He spent six months to a year in Brazil, absorbing what he could about growing and buying green coffee.

Then he went to the Brooklyn plant on Hudson Street, where the whole building was on an angle and Jack Dempsey the roaster was a very important person. Later he convinced his father there should be a green coffee buying office in New York. He opened that office in 1954, hiring John Heuman to head it up. Mr. Heuman had been with a green coffee importing firm. In his new position he reported to Robert Cohn.

Mr. Cohn returned to Chicago, where he assumed responsibility for coffee buying while keeping a hand in on the financial and administrative direction of the company. In 1964 he succeeded his brother Alvin as president of Continental, bringing to the new post "a record of broad experience . . . in every phase of our business," his father said in a letter to employees.

In a matter of months, he began to lead Continental away from coffee as its dominant business to a whole new arena. He began by initiating a process of self-questioning by Continental executives about directions the company should take.

A series of meetings ensued in which Continental leadership began to change the definition of the company from predominantly coffee roasting and distributing to the manufacture and distribution of products and services for the food-service industry.

Years later, in 1979, Robert Cohn initiated yet another process of self-examination, this time by use of strategic planning.

By then the company was transformed to multiline distribution. The question was not what to do but how best to do it — or, as the strategic planner puts it, how best to allocate resources. At this time Mr. Cohn formed a management committee and asked it to work with a consultant. He had been exposed to strategic planning in seminars and wanted his own people to know and use it also.

With growth had come the need to make best use of resources, both financial and human. The planner helped the Continental team understand the need to cut back in some places in order to spend in others. And thus was laid the groundwork, or indeed the strategy, for the '80s.

This strategic planning of another decade obviously is something Jacob Cohn did not engage in. But neither did he engage in the earlier planning of the mid-'60s — not just because he was getting older and had virtually given the company into the hands of his sons, but because he apparently had no concept of planning so systematically so far ahead.

His company was fifty years old in 1965, and he was its honored and beloved founder and inspirational force. But an era ended at the fifty-year mark, if only a few realized it.

Coffee to the Midwest had already given way to Coffee to the Nation, and now Coffee itself was to give way as the dominant commodity. The two Brothers Cohn — Alvin the salesman and his younger brother Robert the planner — were about to lead the company to a new identity and new achievements.

11. SHIFT TO FULL-LINE DISTRIBUTION

In 1964 Alvin Cohn, president of Continental Coffee Company since 1958, paid a consulting firm $25,000 to tell him he should replace himself as president. Mr. Cohn took the advice.

"Tell us what we're doing wrong," he had asked the consultant.

"The truth?" the man asked.

"Yes," said Mr. Cohn.

"You're not in the right job as president," the man said, ticking off the presidential misdemeanors, including an absence of planning, budgeting or meeting with staff.

This came as no news to Mr. Cohn, who knew what he was, a salesman. "I never watched the numbers," he said years later. "I never knew salaries. I never cared about anything but selling."

He asked the man who the president should be and was not surprised to hear the name of his brother Robert, the planner, acutely interested in policy and organization. Robert Cohn became president that year, and Alvin Cohn became vice-chairman.

Meanwhile, the industry was changing. Fast-food and specialty restaurants were multiplying. Workers who once brought their lunch pails were eating in subsidized plant cafeterias. There were more working wives. More people were eating out.

Restaurants became more than just places to eat. Decor began to matter more. Among operators, professionals began to predominate. The owner often enough was a chain. Its management wanted fewer suppliers, better prices, consistent quality and good service in the sense of across-the-board efficiency.

Service as supplied by the route driver-salesman was becoming a luxury. Demand was slipping for high mark-up specialty items. Coffee consumption was down. The days of the specialized distributor were numbered. Robert Cohn saw that the company's growth in this changing industry would call for some careful planning, and he began investigating how a company the size of Continental might answer such a challenge.

After a good deal of study, he decided Continental ought to develop two plans, one for three years and another for five. He knew the development of these plans called for a team effort; so he called a series of meetings of seven top executives. Consultants were retained. Excitement filled the air. The executives asked some basic questions: what business were they in? What kind of company did they have? Where did its future lie?

The executives in addition to Robert were Alvin Cohn, vice-chairman; Stanley Owens, vice-president and managerial factotum for twenty-five years; Louis Leichentritt, specialist in financial matters for the company, an eighteen-year veteran; Dr. Jack Bloom, resident chemist and head of food-processing, another twenty-five-year man; Jim McManus, head of buildings and plants; and Herb Moffatt, director of sales. The meetings extended over six months.

The company was a $50-million-a-year business, ninety percent of it in coffee; but the executives decided after months of discussion that Continental was not a coffee company. It was a foodservice company, a supplier of food and services to people eating away from home.

With this redefinition came the understanding that a new world awaited them if they would remake the company. They could have voted for "battening the hatches and riding it out," as Jack Bloom said years later. But they didn't. Instead, they set objectives for Continental that were incompatible with the company as it then existed — one whose sales were ninety percent coffee.

They would make of Continental a national full-line distributor not only of coffee but of canned and frozen goods, napkins, paper cups — everything a restaurant could use but fresh meat and vegetables and dairy products. They would expand geographically and broaden their production far beyond coffee and "allied" products.

The sons of Jacob Cohn and their associates were creating an industry in response to economic and social change. Jacob Cohn did not fully understand what was happening and remained neutral on the matter.

Among other things, it became clear that the route system would have to go. The company could not continue to compensate route salesmen as they had. Mainly for that reason, it would be increasingly difficult to obtain the same caliber of man for route sales work.

The chains were to be major customers. These looked for a more efficient and less personalized form of sales and delivery. Their buying was already on a more rational, systematized basis.

The business was multiline foodservice. Continental had made its choice. The question was, how go about it? There were two ways. One was to move into a market, buy trucks, hire people, rent a warehouse and start selling — a very expensive proposition which Continental rejected out of hand, though the option was given some consideration in later years.

Instead, Continental bought going concerns and built on them. The first of these was Harmon Foods, Inc, a Memphis, Tennessee, company which it bought in 1967 for only $25,000.

Harmon did not work out, however, and was sold after a loss of about twice the purchase price.

The second effort, also in 1967, was a different story altogether. It was the Keil Company, of Billings, Montana. At the time of its purchase by Continental, Keil was doing $7 million a year business at a profit of one percent. In 1985, after eighteen years of Continental ownership, Keil was doing ten times that amount at a higher rate of profit.

With Keil came a group of managers who helped make it go. Chief among these was Dick Stultz, a young, ambitious and hard-working vice-president. Billings, moreover, was a place where Continental as a company could get experience in full-line distribution, which is what Continental people wanted as much as anything at this point. Billings was a middle-sized city, the sort the company had thrived in for fifty years of "belly to belly" selling, mostly of coffee.

Now sales were to be of much more than coffee. A great shift was under way. Indeed, more than seventy acquisitions were to follow Keil, of which only eight or nine were sold or closed and twenty or so merged with new or existing operations as part of Continental strategy. The rest function profitably as company units. Up to 1967 there had been only fourteen acquisitions — all coffee companies.

Meanwhile, Continental itself was being considered for acquisition by a much bigger company, Super Valu Stores, a Minneapolis-based supplier to the co-op and retail market. Super Valu had a small division called Harrison House, a supplier to the institutional, or foodservice industry.

Super Valu's interest in Continental lay in the role Continental might play in expanding Harrison House. Continental would have taken over that division as part of Super Valu's strategy to grow as a foodservice-industry supplier. Super Valu and Continental both realized that the foodservice industry was going to grow mightily in the years ahead.

The companies would have traded stock for stock. Super

Valu at $750 million a year in sales dwarfed the $100-million-a-year Continental. But twenty-five percent of Super Valu stock would have gone to Continental shareholders, who as the biggest shareholding group would have controlled the bigger company.

The deal would have combined Continental coffee routes in the Twin Cities with Super Valu's wholesale grocery operation, achieving just the mix that Continental was seeking. Robert Cohn would have moved to Minneapolis to head up an expanded foodservice division and to work into management of the retail division as well. The move would have been a way for Continental to enter multiline distribution and for Super Valu to apply its multiline capabilities to the blossoming foodservice industry.

But Jacob Cohn was lukewarm regarding the idea. One can imagine his reluctance at seeing his company swallowed up. When he died in June of 1968, negotiations slowed down. They finally ground to a halt when Robert and Alvin Cohn decided Continental ought to pursue multiline distribution on its own.

Meanwhile, at Keil, a son-in-law of the former owner left the company as he had intended to do, leaving the astute Dick Stultz in charge. Mr. Stultz promptly began the spate of acquisitions that characterized his years at the Keil helm, beginning with Big Red Grocery Company, of Fargo, North Dakota, about which more later.

Continental had no coffee routes in Fargo, which in that respect made it less than ideal. It did in Michigan, however, where Continental made its next acquisition, in which Keil was not involved, and set the stage for implementing its strategy of integrating full-line distribution with coffee routes.

This was the Detroit-based institutional food division of Vlasic Foods. This division was acquired in 1969. Continental had five routes in Detroit and twelve elsewhere in Michigan. The Detroit routes dated from the 1920s, when Al Marans, one of the first Continental salesmen, began selling Continental coffee there. The rest of the state had been opened up in the late 1930s by Gene Irwin, who operated out of Lansing as district sales manager.

Vlasic Foods also ran a retail pickle business, for which the name is probably best known, and was involved in financing and in dairy products. Beginning as a distributor to retail stores, the company at one point had topped $25 million in annual sales. But co-ops had dug into the market, and sales had shrunk. The family had then moved to the institutional (foodservice) business, which at the time of the Continental purchase was doing $5 million to $7 million a year in sales. The Vlasic contact was made by Alvin Cohn, who knew one of the family, Robert Vlasic, through the Young Presidents Organization, of which both were members.

The Vlasic company sold frozen and canned foods but no coffee. Continental sold coffee, but its panel trucks could not carry the Vlasic line. Continental salesmen gave up their trucks and made their calls in cars. Vlasic trucks were used to deliver the now expanded Continental line. One by one, the Continental and Vlasic routes were integrated throughout the state. It was the beginning of full-line distribution in Michigan for Continental. It was also the beginning of the end of the route-sales era.

The coffee route business was on its way out anyhow. As restaurants switched to automatic brewers, urn-cleaning services were no longer as much needed. These new brewers, commonly called Silex, were made of glass, as opposed to urns, which were made of metal. Weekly delivery of coffee was no longer as much needed either, especially for small accounts, since packaging had advanced to the point where freshness could be assured without it.

The full-line salesman brewed coffee for a taste test far less frequently than his route-sales predecessors had, because coffee became a minor aspect of his sales effort. Instead he showed the customer items in a thick, catalog-like book. Selling from and by the book was in.

Continental's acquisitions were taking it into an industry that organizationally speaking was in a fairly elementary state. Most wholesalers were not well equipped with managers. Most were family-owned and "did their accounting by pencil," to quote Aaron Clark, financial advisor to the Cohns.

Robert Cohn realized the need for professional managers. It was an abiding concern for him. He himself functions in a highly organized fashion, as Howard Koven, the firm's chief counsel, testifies. Mr. Koven recalls how demanding his many sessions have been with Mr. Cohn and how well prepared he had to be for them. The two would drive downtown together and in forty-five minutes would handle matters that in most circumstances would require several hours.

Alvin Cohn's style, on the other hand, was that of a salesman and a marketing man. While Robert was working through problems of strategy and organization, Alvin was out persuading foodservice industry customers that Continental could best meet their needs.

Indeed, it was Alvin who had almost singlehandedly brought Continental into the national markets that were crucial to pursuit of the full-line distribution strategy. As a young man just out of service after World War II, he had cultivated and sold the chains, including Szabo Food Services, Holiday Inns and ARA Services.

By his efforts he had shown the Continental sales force they should not be afraid to go after big accounts. Later it was his contacts in the International Foodservice Manufacturing Association that helped Continental leadership realize what was happening in the industry. Both he and Robert Cohn served as president of this organization. Spurred on by this awareness, Continental set the stage for the strategizing that led to its big shift.

As the shift moved ahead, Alvin Cohn for a time promoted

the goal of one-stop service, by which the Continental truck would supply everything a customer needed in one call. It was an ideal not to be reached, however, because restaurants' needs were too diverse.

Thus Continental distribution was full-line in the sense that it did all one company could do for a full-service restaurant — meet about seventy-five percent of its needs. It did not supply produce or milk, for instance. In a sense a better word for it would be "multiline."

Fast-food, limited menu restaurants, on the other hand, were one-stop customers. Either the supplier brought them what they needed, or they didn't have it and they were in big trouble. They had no room to improvise.

"Did you ever go to a McDonald's and find there were no French fries?" asks Stan Owens, who headed Continental's sales and distribution operation in the early '70s.

The shift to full-line went pretty much as Robert Cohn and the others planned, except that it cost more and took longer than they thought it would. But it was an exhilarating experience, in effect the creation of an industry. The Continental team set up goals that were "attainable, realistic and challenging" (A-R-C for short), and for the most part achieved them.

In 1976 and 1977, however, some chickens came home briefly to roost .The company's growth began to produce problems, especially in controls. The volume got out of hand, given Continental's management structure and level of managerial expertise.

Robert Cohn found himself besieged with doubts. Had they gone too far, too soon? In the middle of a down year, the company's first, he was finding it a depressing experience and began to lose confidence. It he couldn't recover his confidence, he decided, he might have to resign, for the good of the company. Unburdening himself at lunch one day to Solomon Dutka, a Continental director, he found himself on the defensive.

"Who are you not to have a down year? Sears and General Motors have them. Why not you?" Mr. Dutka asked. He reproached Robert Cohn for feeling that he was immune to a temporary setback. The tactic worked. Mr. Cohn rethought his position, took Mr. Dutka's words to heart and stayed to fight another day.

The shift to full-line distribution produced radical changes in the Continental profile. Coffee sales dropped to 8% of total sales by 1983, from 90% in 1965. Geographical coverage was national, in contrast to heavy Middle West and Northeast U. S. concentration in 1971, when those areas accounted for 65% of sales.

While the Middle West and Northeast business was shrinking to 34%, the Far West share of Continental business was more than doubling during these twelve years, from 15% to 37%. The other big market shift was to the South, which rose from 6% to 16% of Continental sales. In the region between the Mississippi River and the Rocky Mountains, the share rose from 14% to 18%.

From 1978, the year after the 1977 slump, to 1983, financial figures rose sharply. Sales, assets and equity each increased more than 60%, invested capital more than 40%, working capital 23%, but total debt only 19%. Net debt dropped more than 5%. Revenues rose from $698 million to $1.1 billion, net income from $5.4 million to $16 million. Earnings per share rose from 61 cents to $1.87. The figures make the planning sessions of 1965 look good.

12. KEIL AND WHAT FOLLOWED

Once Continental decided to go full-distribution to the foodservice industry, it was a matter, we have seen, of buying properties that would help that process along. The Keil Company, in Billings, Montana, the first such purchase that worked, provided the key to Continental's move into full-line distribution.

Dick Stultz came with the Keil company. He had joined it as a truck driver right out of high school, at eighteen. Then he had run the warehouse and sold for fifteen years. When Continental bought the company in 1967, he was credit and sales manager. Bob Buchanan, the owner, told Continental not to worry, Dick Stultz could run the place. He was right about that.

Working under Stan Owens, president of the newly established sales and distribution division, now foodservice division, Mr. Stultz not only took over Keil but also inspired further acquisitions. His plan, cleared with Robert Cohn, was to acquire successful companies which he could supervise from Billings while they were operated by the same managers as before. They had to be close enough to Billings to allow this. Each of these new companies would be points on spokes of a wheel, with Billings its hub.

The first of these, in 1968, was Big Red Grocery Company, in Fargo, North Dakota, owned by the Litovsky brothers, immigrants from Russia. One of these, Max, chose to retire, and the other Ben, stayed on after the sale to do yeoman work.

Big Red commanded half the area's wholesale business, doing its selling by telephone, with same-day delivery. The Litovskys were personally involved as buyers, salesmen and credit managers, serving schools, restaurants and hospitals. Ben Litovsky greatly impressed his peers on the Continental sales force with his savvy.

The J. P. Michael Company in Indianopolis, a 1969 acquisition, was a case of inflation overtaking the owners' ability to finance the enterprise. The owners were Billy Meyer, a grandson of the founder, and his brother-in-law, Fritz Goldbach. They had to sell when the cost of their inventory and receivables rose and they borrowed beyond their ability to repay their loans. It was that or cut sales back drastically, and they weren't willing to do that.

J. P. Michael offered Continental the chance to try out its strategy of merging coffee routes into full-line distribution. In business for more than seventy-five years, it had an excellent reputation for the quality of its products and service. Continental coffee, on the other hand, was probably the largest selling coffee in the state. Its reputation was tops, and its sales force, developed over the years by the acknowledged dean of Continental sales managers, Bernard Pippenger, was outstanding.

The opportunity was too good to pass up. The acquisition made, the integration of coffee routes with J. P. Michael's routes was begun, first in Indianapolis and then throughout the state, in phases, inevitable problems notwithstanding. In the end, Continental salesmen left their routes and their delivery trucks in favor of autos. Deliveries were made in big trucks by others while they reverted to a strictly sales function, with thousands more items to sell than before. A major learning process was in order for them, of course, as to a much lesser extent for the J. P. Michael salesmen, who added coffee and the allied line to their already huge stock of items for sale. This was the Continental strategy, to add hundreds of products to its sales inventory. J. P. Michael salesmen for their part now had coffee and specialty food products to sell to their customers. This exchange, it was reasoned, would increase sales substantially, and that's what happened, though somewhat slower than expected.

But a disagreement arose between Billy Meyer and Stan Owens about what constituted a reasonable profit margin, and Mr. Meyer left the company, though on friendly terms. He held out for the 1% margin on which he and his father and grandfather before him had operated the company and in which he passionately believed. Mr. Owens, on the other hand, intended to aim for a higher margin, convinced that without it growth would be very difficult to attain. His program called for cost-cutting, concentration on higher-margin items, and selling more items per customer.

Southern Institutional Foods, in Houston, another 1969 purchase, turned out to be a mistake. The company was too small and ranked near the bottom in area sales. On top of that, the sellers after the sale went into the spice business as competitors.

Not the seller's son, however, a deputy sheriff who thought so highly of this role that he presented himself at a branch manager's meeting in Chicago wearing a gun in a holster — the first branch manager to appear that way and probably the last as well. He later left the company. Continental's practice since this Houston experience is to buy only companies that rank either first or second in their marketing areas.

Tableware Corporation, of Skokie, Illinois, a 1970 acquisition from Mort Selz, was considered very important, especially by Alvin Cohn, because it put Continental into the business of selling dining-out equipment. Equipment sales, Alvin reasoned, would open the door to more business (food and equipment deliveries could be simultaneous) and would provide a better margin than food alone. Tableware was integrated with Continental. Mr. Selz, who had worked years earlier for Continental as an office boy, became vice-president-sales for equipment and supplies.

Meanwhile, another Billings company, Warehouse Markets, was bought in 1970. A discount operation, formerly part of Keil, it looked good because Bob Buchanan, the former Keil president, strongly favored this sort of company and Dick Stultz felt it would make a good outlet for slow-moving or damaged Keil merchandise. But Continental later sold Warehouse Markets after considering and then rejecting the idea of starting a chain of discount outlets. The idea was judged too much a departure from Continental's main enterprise.

E. J. Byman & Company, in Calumet City, southeast of Chicago, was also bought in 1970. It had a nice facility, and its owners were ready to retire. One stayed with the business, however. This man proved a good teacher for Continental's director of personnel, Joe Kennedy, who asked for a line management job and was assigned to Byman. Mr. Kennedy remained there until Byman was absorbed into the Rosemont facility near O'Hare airport.

Another Stultz-instigated acquisition, in a resort and ranching area, was Panetta Brothers Distributing Company, in Sheridan, Wyoming, in 1971. Panetta Brothers served mostly a summertime clientele, but the Sheridan area was branching out to winter activities, with the promise of increased business. Ron McArthur, transferred from Billings, ran it until it was merged with the Billings operation, according to Mr. Stultz's plan at the time of the acquisition.

In 1971 another acquisition, in the Indianapolis area, put Continental further into equipment and supplies, this time on a national basis. National China and Equipment Corporation, in Marion, Indiana, was bought from the Maidenberg brothers, one of whom was in failing health and wanted to retire. The other, Milt Maidenberg, stayed on. Their company had a very good reputation in the business, as did Milt Maidenberg himself. Moreover, as Tableware, a regional operation, put Continental into the equipment business, National China put Continental into it nationally and gave it a much wider selection of merchandise. Milt Maidenberg was put in charge of Continental's equipment-supply organization. When he left Continental a few years later, his able right-hand man Jim Shildmeyer took over.

Central Florida Foods, Inc., in Sanford, Florida, near Orlando, was bought in 1971 as a way of gaining entree into Florida with full-line distribution. It was a small, $2-million-a-year business owned by two partners, one of whom wanted to be free to work full-time as a traveling evangelist. The other, an easygoing man in charge of sales, Lyman Philips, wanted to stay.

Paul Eibert and Stan Owens hesitated, because the plant was small. But Mr. Owens was eager to get into Florida and there was little risk in the deal; so Continental went ahead with it. The operation prospered, requiring in time a new facility. The company grew with the area and today has annual sales of about $40 million.

Another Stultz acquisition about this time was Crystal Distributing Company, in Duluth, Minnesota, where Continental had coffee routes. As a company within the ample Billings orbit (859 miles away), Crystal fit into the regional strategy which Mr. Stultz was pursuing. As one with ready access to Continental coffee customers, it fit into Continental's national strategy of integrating its routes with food wholesalers. Continental was in Minneapolis as well, and this made the Crystal acquisition even more attractive. Isidore "Izzie" Crystal and "Prof" Davis were its principals. Both were good at what they did — Mr. Crystal as a salesman, Mr. Davis as an inside man responsible for warehouse and trucks, both of them as buyers. Mr. Davis retired when Continental bought the company, but Mr. Crystal stayed through the '70s, running the operation.

A 1971 acquisition that particularly elicited the Cohn brothers' enthusiasm was United Food Service Supply Company, of St. Paul. Alone among Continental acquisitions at this time, United was doing full-line distribution to a number of customers, rather than to a few big ones. It was the kind of business the Cohns wanted very much to get into, and they coveted the expertise, well known to them, of United's principals, Harold Neifeld and Mickey Bearman, who had developed and made a success of this concept pretty much from scratch. With their help, the Cohns planned to lead their other branches into the same business. United kept its name for two years after its acquisition, so fully established was it in full-line distribution, even including dairy products.

Two years later, in 1973, Continental acquired Oken Supreme, Inc., in Golden Valley, a Minneapolis suburb. Oken, the product of a two-company merger only eighteen months earlier, was in possession of a modern, one-story building which itself was very attractive for the efficiency it promised. United Food Service Supply, whose multi-story building was old and relatively inefficient, was merged into Oken. Jerry Wagner, the Keil controller, a typically good Stultz management find, took over this newly combined operation, which became profitable after a few lean years.

During the early '70s, Keil in Billings did the Fargo, Duluth, Twin Cities and Des Moines operations' bookkeeping, in addition to its own. Des Moines was home for Hoxie Institutional Wholesale Company, which had branches in Waterloo and Dubuque. Eventually, all of Iowa was merged into one big Des Moines building, thanks to the computerized system in that city.

The Hoxie owner was a man along in years and not in good health who therefore wanted to sell — a typical acquisition situation for Continental. His general manager, Eugene Van Vleet, a man of about thirty-five, was also sales manager. Continental, with five or six coffee routes already in Iowa, acquired Hoxie with a view to the Des Moines consolidation.

Acquisitions continued through the '70s in implementation of the full-service strategy. In 1972, in line with a concurrent strategy of moving into areas of fast population growth, Continental looked closely at PM Foods, Inc., in Phoenix, Arizona. A move into fast-growing Arizona appealed mightily to Stan Owens, now heading sales and distribution. But PM was smaller than he liked; so he hesitated, even if Arizona beckoned so strongly. He and his assistant in charge of plants, Glenn Tobin, visited the PM facility. They found it as small as they had been told, but they were impressed by PM's general manager, a thirty-year industry veteran. The GM planned to retire in a year or so, but he said he would train a replacement; so Continental went ahead with the acquisition.

Meanwhile, Alvin Cohn had recommended a young man right out of college to work on the Denver route system. This was Robert Nussbaum, who was working under Ben Kristopeit's tutelage. But route sales were on the way out, and Mr. Nussbaum needed experience in full-line distribution. The Phoenix situation with its built-in training aspect appeared ideal for this. Mr. Nussbaum went there and after a year or so took over as branch manager.

The same year, 1972, Continental acquired Polunsky's Inc., of San Antonio, a distributor of fish and other frozen products run by three brothers. Their father had started it as a retail fish store, which the family still operated. The seafood market looked good to Continental, which already had coffee routes in San Antonio. In addition, the frozen line looked expandable. A facility could be built or acquired later to house route merchandise and frozen products. Continental could add dry groceries to the mix and have a full-line operation in San Antonio, the thinking went. Continental bought Polunsky's. But Sam Polunsky, ablest of the three brothers, retired after a year. Building a facility, furthermore, was ruled out as too expensive, and finding one proved difficult. So consolidation plans were scrapped, and Continental sold Polunsky's back to the family.

Dayton (Ohio) Frozen Foods, Inc., was bought that year for its good reputation, its location and its product line, which included some non-frozen items. The company was well located to take advantage of Continental's extensive coffee-route system in Ohio, for one thing. For another, Dayton was close enough to Indianapolis to be managed from that city, a long-time prosperous Continental sales hub. Indeed, Dayton's buying and credit operations could be run from Indianapolis, the reasoning went, with obvious savings. This in fact is what happened.

Meanwhile, Alvin Cohn had been probing the question of fast-food/limited-menu restaurants and their rise within the industry. About this time it became clear that fast food was growing more rapidly than foodservice as a whole. The trend was up and would continue to be up for the foreseeable future. The indicated strategy for Continental was clear enough — to acquire well-established fast-food/limited-menu foodservice companies. The strategy was to work well, providing Continental a foothold in this facet of foodservice and setting it head and shoulders above its competitors. Security analysts were to pay special attention to this breakthrough by Continental to leadership in foodservice's fastest-growing operation.

Thus in 1972 Continental acquired a Chicago-based shortening-maker, Interstate Foods Corporation, which supplied McDonald's. Interstate had developed a product in the early years of fast-food which McDonald's chose for use in processing its French fries. As McDonald's had grown, so had Interstate, establishing a national presence with plants in Chicago and in Vernon, California. Harry Smargon, co-owner of Interstate, was well known to Alvin Cohn and Stan Owens from his years in the coffee business in Chicago. Ken Smargon, Harry's son, was moving to succeed his father as head of Interstate. He remained for some time after the sale running the company.

In the following year, 1973, Continental bought another distributor of fast-food shortening, Philadelphia Refining & Packaging Company, in Camden, New Jersey. The acquisition gave Continental a shortening producer and distributor in the East to go with those it already had in California and Chicago — the two Interstate Foods operations. Interstate was already shipping to the East Coast. The New Jersey acquisition gave it an Eastern base for its growing Eastern accounts, including the national chains.

The same year, Continental acquired a third equipment-and-supply company, after Tableware and National China — Imperial Arts Corporation, in the northwest Chicago suburb of Elk Grove Village, near O'Hare airport. Like National China, Imperial Arts was a national operation, but it added an important dimension, namely the distribution of imported items, mainly from the Far East. The firm also distributed domestic items, but it seemed to have especially good connections in Japan and Korea. One of the two principal owners, Irwin Schneider, young and aggressive, ran the business. Mr. Garland, the majority owner, remained primarily an investor.

Shortly thereafter, Continental's vice-president for acquisitions, Paul Eibert, got together with George Barnett and Bill Harper in Macon, Georgia. Mr. Barnett was major owner of two companies, Mulberry Provision Company in downtown Macon and Institutional Wholesalers, Inc., on the city's outskirts. Mr. Harper operated the latter company. Both men impressed Mr. Eibert. Later Mr. Owens met them and was equally impressed. Mr. Barnett's father had come to Macon from New York City and opened a butcher shop which became a full-fledged provision company and then a full-line distributor.

The last expansion called for more space, and that's when the firm had opened its new, modern facility on the edge of town. There had been steady growth and there was good management depth with a high market share when Continental looked the two companies over. They shook hands on a deal.

But while papers were being drawn up, word got out about the sale, and a competitor offered Mr. Barnett a higher price. Though not legally bound, Mr. Barnett declined the higher offer, telling the competitor his handshake was as good as a signed document. Over several years thereafter of working with Mr. Barnett, Continental executives found cause only to verify that claim further. Bill Harper and "Red" Strong, another of the Macon group, continued to run both operations, also to Continental's satisfaction, and they do so to this day.

During 1975 Continental further implemented its strategic plan calling for penetration of all major U. S. markets, buying a company near Pittsburgh and another near Atlanta. The one near Pittsburgh was Topper Food Distributors, Inc., in Eighty-four, Pennsylvania. The principal owner, Ralph Gruber, was a food-distribution veteran who had formed Topper after some years in the employ of a major local distributor. He was selling because of his growing need for capital. The Topper acquisition gave Continental full-line distribution in the eastern part of its marketing area. Mr. Gruber stayed on to run Continental-Topper.

The other 1975 acquisition, Atlanta Grocery Company, Inc., in Doraville, Georgia, gave Continental the Southeastern U. S. base it was seeking, and in one of the country's fastest-growing areas. The big Doraville facility was new, and the outlay connected with its construction had put a dent in Atlanta Grocery Company's financial condition. But the acquisition went through anyhow — not for cash but for Continental convertible preferred stock. This arrangement permitted the sellers to participate in Continental's growth as shown in the value of its common stock, while at the same time gaining assurance of regular income from the preferred stock.

Meanwhile, the candy business beckoned — not to satisfy a Continental sweet tooth but because its management committee saw confectionery as a growth industry that could be tied to institutional foodservice. In 1976 Continental bought Shari Candies Inc., in Mankato, Minnesota, which had a division in Shorewood, Wisconsin, just outside Milwaukee, called Barg & Foster. Shari was primarily a "bagger" of candies, mainly for retail distribution. Barg & Foster did manufacturing for Shari but also had customers of its own. Again, Continental convertible preferred stock was the medium of exchange, with its guaranteed return and option to realize the rising value of Continental common stock.

Continental's goal was to test the waters of this industry by buying a fairly small operation. The testing process continued with the purchase in the same year of Melster Candies, in Cambridge, Wisconsin, another small company with a somewhat different product mix. Shari and Melster worked together profitably for a number of years, but the fit with Continental's major business did not materialize, nor was their growth sufficient to justify Continental's involvement. Both companies were sold during 1983 and 1984.

In 1977 Continental made an acquisition which increased its access to the increasingly important fast-food market. This was the Sugar Food Corporation, in Columbus, Ohio, a highly regarded distributor to fast-food restaurants including Rax and Wendy's. Rax operates in Southeastern and Midwestern U.S. Sugar Food had been one of the first full-line distributors to fast-food outlets and was highly regarded by operators. Its manager, Joseph Sugar, greatly impressed Continental's team.

Sugar Food's line was as limited as its customers' menus; but each of its highly specialized items was of crucial importance to the operator, from hamburger meat to ketchup. Ready availability of merchandise was imperative. This requirement called for good buying contacts and efficient handling of inventory. Margins in servicing the fast-food industry were lower than in full-line; but turnover was fast, payment was prompt and individual deliveries were for much higher dollar amounts.

In 1979 Continental entered a niche with the acquisition of Chicago-based Houston Foods, Ltd., which assembles and distributes holiday food gift packages to department stores mostly between Thanksgiving and Christmas. Houston customers included prestige stores such as Marshall Field's and Macy's and big chains such as Sears, Ward's and K-Mart.

The founder, Mickey Houston, was well known to the Cohns and Stanley Owens because of his thirty-five or so years in food distribution. The Houston family's produce business, Sam Houston & Sons, still is operating. Mr. Houston had branched out on his own with this specialized gift-package business in 1952, had done well at it and had sold it to J. M. Smucker Company in 1971. But the Smucker relationship became strained, and Mr. Houston came to his friends at Continental to see if they would like to buy the business. They did so in 1979, judging it to fit with their full-line distribution. Mr. Houston stayed on as president of Houston Foods until his death in 1985.

In 1981 Continental bought a San Francisco-area distributor which was not only well managed and number-one in its market area but for Continental very well located. Northern California was of particular interest to Continental because its many Los Angeles customers frequently had outlets in the north which they wanted Continental to serve. Some prospective customers, in fact, had told Continental they could have their business only if Continental would also serve their northern California outlets.

The company — Avard-Garth, in Union City — was a division of Distribuco, Inc., which had bought it after earlier negotiations by Continental had fallen through. Avard-Garth had been privately held during those earlier negotiations. Continental bought it from Distribuco in 1981 and thus gained its northern California base. It also gained a top-flight management team, which General Manager Jack Schaefer had developed and which agreed to stay on with the new owner. Thus the acquisition not only followed the Continental strategy of multiline market penetration. It also contributed richly to the firm's management mix. Indeed, in a short time it was necessary to add substantial freezer space to the Avard-Garth facility to accommodate business growth and to provide its busy sales force with an adequate variety of frozen products.

Also in 1981, Continental acquired the Chicago-area foodservice business (salesmen, customers, inventory, receivables) of the PYA Monarch division of Consolidated Foods, which decided to withdraw from the area. Monarch made the contact, saying they felt Continental was best qualified to handle their business. Continental acquired no physical facilities in the deal.

With the Monarch receivables came guarantee of payment. The integration of customers and salesmen at the Rosemont plant took some doing, since it involved numerous details. But the Rosemont plant's financial results were eventually helped by the addition of the Monarch business.

In 1982 Continental entered the Miami, Florida, market with the acquisition of the Miami division of International Food Service. Florida as the nation's fastest growing state was an obvious target area. Continental was already in Miami and up to Palm Beach with its coffee routes, not to mention its established full-line presence since 1971 in Orlando. Security analysts continued in their praise of Continental's moves to Sun Belt markets. So there was no doubt that a strong move to full-line distribution in the Miami area was a natural.

In the same year, Continental bought a Philadelphia-area fast-food distributor, Foodservice Specialists, Inc., of Mechanicsburg, Pennsylvania, owned by a highly respected foodservice veteran, Al Walsh. Foodservice Specialists had recently moved into a new facility, which with Mr. Walsh's acknowledged expertise made the company a very attractive buy. The location was excellent, in a major highly concentrated metropolitan area where Continental already had fast-food customers. An increase in volume was firmly expected.

Also in 1982 Continental bought Portland (Oregon) Wholesale Grocery Company from International Foodservice, thus filling the last gap in its coverage of major West Coast markets. The Lamprose brothers, sons of the founder, were PWG's well-respected owners and operators. Continental management knew they knew their business and welcomed them onto the Continental team. With their entering the fold, Portland became Continental's fifth major West Coast outlet, with Los Angeles, San Francisco, San Diego and Seattle. There was an added benefit to this acquisition: Continental's Seattle branch had business in Portland, as PWG did in Seattle. The two branches exchanged customers over time, with resultant lessening of travel between the two cities and increased efficiency without loss of volume.

The foodservice division of Alterman Foods Company, in Atlanta, Georgia, was the next acquisition. Alterman approached Continental about selling this division, which was very small compared to the rest of the Alterman operation, which was primarily retail. Continental acquired Alterman's sales force, whatever inventory was of use to Continental, and accounts receivable with Alterman's guarantee it would take back what wasn't collected in six months. The Alterman operation was integrated into Continental-Atlanta, giving a nice boost to its volume and profitability.

In 1983 Continental increased its commitment to the produce business, which it had only occasionally pursued, when it acquired Publix Fruit & Produce, of Seattle. Continental management, especially Alvin and Robert Cohn, had been exploring foodservice industry trends regarding fresh fruits and vegetables. Burger King, Wendy's and other fast-food chains had installed salad bars, and many full-menu restaurants had increased their emphasis on fresh fruits and vegetables.

Several Continental branches were handling produce, but mainly as a continuance of what their business was when Continental acquired them. Publix, a major Seattle produce operation, gave Continental specialized expertise in this area.

Another 1983 acquisition further contributed to Continental's produce business but with a twist. William Callif & Sons, of Columbus, Ohio, distributed exclusively to fast-food operators. Continental management asked, why not use Callif as a supplier to Columbus-based Sugar Food, which by then had been six years in the Continental fold as a fast-food industry distributor? Joe Sugar thought it was a great idea. Shortly after the acquisition, Callif started supplying Sugar Food with produce while continuing to service its own customers — all of this under Mr. Sugar's supervision. Callif later moved into a bigger, more modern facility. The move was a natural fit. Sugar Food's line meshed perfectly with the fast-food produce distributed by Callif.

Continental added a full-line Eastern branch in 1985 with the acquisition of Smelkinson Brothers, a Baltimore foodservice distributor with annual sales of over $100 million. Smelkinson, a well-managed company with good sales and earnings growth, gave Continental a solid base for building up its relatively small Eastern-market penetration. More importantly, the acquisition meant the addition to the Continental team of two top-flight managers, Bob Smelkinson and Sheldon Roth. Both enjoyed splendid reputations among foodservicers for having developed one of the fastest-growing and most efficient distribution companies in the East.

In November of the same year, another produce company joined the Continental fold — Garden Products, of Portland, Oregon. Garden Products was expected to work in handily with Continental's full-line operation, which was so strengthened by the PWG acquisition in 1982.

These final purchases bring up to date the remaking of Continental from a coffee company to a full-line distributor. At the beginning of this historic shift, as we have seen, was the Keil Company and Dick Stultz. In a sense, Mr. Stultz was midwife to the birth of Continental as a full-line distributor. As such, he is a resident expert on how full-line distribution works. Asked to explain it, he had a number of observations.

First of all, full-line distribution is not selling canned goods out of the rear of an old truck. There was a time, as recently as fifteen years ago, when a distributor could start that way, but no more. The distribution business once required little more than hard work. Now it takes expertise and capital as well.

Volume is one problem. The full-line distributor handles between 5,000 and 10,000 items, from soup to napkins. CFS Continental's product catalog is 200 pages long. For Keil this meant growing from $7 million to $55 million in annual sales between 1967 and 1985. It achieved this growth while servicing a two-state area, Montana and Wyoming, in which it came to command a very high market share of 12% to 15%.

Success came because of Keil's bigger and better organization and sales force, at the expense of the smaller distributor. The industry changed, and Keil changed with it. Keil was acquired with a view to expansion; so this comes as no surprise.

Changes are still being made. Keil is doing more business with Kentucky Fried Chicken and other chains which in less concentrated areas like Billings do not have their dedicated supply centers. But even now, as he did for years as president of Keil, Mr. Stultz visits customers when he senses that both salesman and customer want him to. So did Jacob Cohn, who as founder-president of Continental Coffee Company was in regular touch with dozens of customers.

With size come problems. Of every 1,500 cases on a truck, for instance, probably ten or fifteen were misordered or were dropped and damaged. The driver might have dropped a case and broken it. If the damage is messy, the case goes to the garbage. The customer is credited, messy or not, of course. It it's a case of the wrong goods, the driver returns them to the plant.

Keil makes a unique use of its seven over-the-road trucks (nine in the busy summer months). Those making the Chicago run, to pick goods up from the Continental warehouse for distribution, haul wheat on the way there. They make this trip every three weeks.

In the other direction, to West Coast canneries, they make fifteen trips a week, again hauling wheat on the way. Keil has been doing this type of hauling since 1948. The whole business is coordinated by the head buyer. Trucking in this sense was once a very profitable part of the business. Even now this kind of hauling is profitable.

As for the sales process itself, there are three ways to get new customers: solve a customer's problem, become his friend, and reduce prices.

Price-reduction is a matter of offering a special item, reduced almost to cost. The company can afford this on one item, at least for a while. The sale puts a customer's name on an invoice. This is an important first step. Selling shortening as a special, for instance, the salesman comes every week. He probably begins to sell more than the special, and this starts a relationship.

The customer begins to depend on some special services the salesman renders, as getting napkins or taco shells when he runs out. The salesman might buy them from one of his competitors if necessary. Mr. Stultz has had items flown in from Seattle when matters got critical. Or he has hustled to obtain a substitute brand, as of pickles or French fries if he ran out of them for a regular customer.

He can't always use a substitute brand, however. Some are "never-never-out" items, as monogrammed napkins for the popular Golden Belle Restaurant in Billings. Such a place demands its own napkins. Another customer might accept a plain substitute napkin once, but not again. Whoever the customer, it's very important to keep inventory up to meet the customer's demands.

A full-line supplier is one that meets a high percentage of a restaurant's needs. As for having just one supplier, a hundred-percent supplier, there are advantages for the customer but disadvantages too. This applies to the distributor as well as his customer, of course.

It is more efficient to be called on by just one salesman rather than several, to have one delivery and to be billed only once. But there are problems with depending on one supplier. Having more than one enables you to check on the others, "keep 'em honest," as Mr. Stultz says.

Mr. Stultz buys sliced American and Swiss cheese, for instance. But he won't "get in bed" with either of two cheese suppliers. Instead he buys Swiss from one and American from the other.

A salesman normally wants all of a customer's business. But he still might appreciate a little competition, say by a small jobber who handles ten percent of a big customer's business. This is ideal, in fact. The small operation does not compete with the full-line distributor in this case but complements the full-line distributor as a backup supplier.

For his salespeople, Mr. Stultz generally hires young men (a few women too) who have worked in the business, as in bread or beer delivery or as a fast-food chef. He starts them in the warehouse (as Jacob Cohn used to start them in the shipping room). Then he puts them to riding with a delivery truck driver, and then to the "city desk," where orders are taken, to learn products, customers and the like.

This takes three or four months. Then they are put on relief sales work and after that are eligible for territories of their own. At any given time, someone is in training and someone is on vacation or otherwise in need of relief; so it works out. People quit or retire too, of course.

All in all, Mr. Stultz experiences about twenty percent annual turnover in the Billings sales force — say, five a year out of twenty-five. New sales territories are split off from existing ones when volume justifies it. The man taking on a new (split) territory is usually given a six-month wages guarantee, which can be extended. Salesmen sometimes suggest the split themselves, when their work load is getting out of hand.

As for buyers, they simply "emerge," Mr. Stultz says. Some are salesmen who don't like to travel. The buyer has a thankless job. Salesmen complain about things, and indeed a lot can go wrong: truckers might be late, material might be out of stock in the warehouse. It's a big week for peaches, and they run out before demand is met. Crop shortages happen. It's all blamed on the buyer.

It's up to the buyer to manage "turns," or turnovers, of his stock so that they occur in time to sell almost all of an order just as the next is coming in. It isn't easy. Commodities differ widely in frequency of turnover. There should be twelve a year for canned peaches, for instance, but two a week for eggs.

The buyer gets stock status reports daily and weekly. He is told about abnormal movements of stock, but that doesn't mean he can always do something about them. Achieving the right mix in a warehouse-bound truckload is like fitting pieces into a puzzle. There are forty kinds of Kellogg's cereal, for instance. The buyer must decide how many of what kind to order. And he orders some things before the last order has arrived.

He uses a computer to keep track but checks on computer-originated figures by cycle or spot handcounting. Many people are involved in the process, and for every one there is an increased chance of error.

A picker might pick the wrong item. The buyer might

punch an order for 11 (eleven) cases into the computer when the order was for 1 (one). The salesman sends 10 cases back, and the buyer thinks he sold them and orders more. An experienced night clerk will catch that sort of thing. As in anything else, you can't beat experience.

Continental expansion which followed on the Keil acquisition was a fitting together of working parts of a huge machine. There were parts within parts, however, and in this sense the role of California looms large. Let us look then at how growth in California served Continental strategy in the 1960s, 1970s and 1980s.

13. CALIFORNIA

Continental Coffee Company entered California in 1960, when Frank Hoffmann began selling in Los Angeles to a market that did not appreciate his wares. He had sold coffee in the Midwest and in Denver, relishing competition when success depended on how good his product was. In California, on the other hand, it wasn't what he was selling that made the difference but how much equipment he was ready to lend.

The realization struck him with depressing clarity when he was told by a prospective customer that even though the prospective's present coffee was perhaps only so-so, he wasn't interested in changing brands. If he did, the prospect would say, he'd have to buy his own coffeemaker and/or waitress station or even the booths his patrons sat in.

The rub, of course, was that the prospect's present coffee, unsatisfactory as it might be, was sold to him by a company that loaned out all that equipment on condition he buy its coffee. All the restaurant owner had to do to lose that coffeemaker or waitress station or booths (tagged with the real owner's name) was to start buying Continental coffee instead of the equipment-owner's brand.

These were not the best of times for Frank Hoffmann. Continental policy was adamantly opposed to buying business with equipment. The most it would do in this direction was to sell coffeemakers at a low $2 a week charge to the customer until the total was paid. Continental would not countenance hidden costs of loaned equipment.

Not that Mr. Hoffmann wanted to do that. He wanted to sell coffee on its merits, but that wasn't easy in Los Angeles. Standards differed. No restaurant in Los Angeles won the Gold Cup, for instance — the award given by the National Coffee Association for serving excellent coffee. He was able to persuade a few restaurateurs to make coffee a priority. But in general, Los Angeles and the rest of California made an average coffee market at best for Continental.

But Mr. Hoffmann and his deliveryman Dick Holsclaw stuck it out — Mr. Hoffmann in a sedan and Mr. Holsclaw in a truck. The driver salesman was still the rule, but in Los Angeles they did it this way.

The company still wanted that California market. A foothold was needed. You couldn't start out of the rear of Dick Holsclaw's truck. You needed some sort of facility to begin to compete successfully with the equipment-lenders.

The first effort at acquiring a facility was unsuccessful. Stan Owens, in Seattle, was asked by Jacob Cohn to stop by Los Angeles on his way back to Chicago. There was a Mr. Moseley in Los Angeles who owned a coffee company and wanted to sell.

Mr.Owens called Mr. Moseley for an appointment and was asked to meet him in Palm Springs, where Mr. Moseley would make the company's audit reports and other papers available to him. This he did, and the two met and discussed the matters.

It was Breakfast Club Coffee Company that was for sale. Mr. Moseley wanted out of the business. He was up in years, had a heart condition and no longer had an appetite for the fuss and strain. "Is he our type of businessman?" Mr. Cohn asked by telephone from Chicago after Mr. Owens and Mr. Moseley met.

He was indeed, but there were other considerations that kiboshed the deal. Alvin Cohn discovered them on a later trip; salesmen mostly up in years, an aged truck fleet and customers consisting largely of small accounts.

Instead, in that same year, 1962, Continental bought for $300,000 a company consisting almost entirely of a small, two-story coffee plant in rented quarters on San Fernando Road in Glendale, outside Los Angeles. A young man in his thirties, Jack Archer, was running that business, which was mostly private-label but included some foodservice customers as well.

The Glendale plant had only one roaster and little space in which to store either green or roasted coffee. Two Continental veterans were sent there from the Midwest as hopes ran high to make Glendale a jumping-off point for the California market — general sales manager Walter Belinky from Chicago as branch manager and district sales manager Kenny Babb from Champaign, Illinois.

Mr. Babb, a tall former Air Corps officer and a very successful salesman, jumped at the chance to go west. But like Frank Hoffmann before him, he found the California experience difficult. He and Mr. Belinky were to work together with the route salesmen, but this arrangement didn't work out.

In a matter of months, Mr. Babb, frustrated by an unaccustomed lack of sales success, by his and Mr. Belinky's inability to work together and by what he saw as lack of understanding by the Chicago office, reached a breaking point.

Upset, he called Stan Owens and told him he wanted to come to Chicago to speak his mind to Jacob Cohn and to resign. "Tell him it never pays to burn your bridges behind you," Mr. Cohn advised when Mr. Owens told him of Mr. Babb's resentful feelings and set up the appointment. Stan Owens did pass on this advice to Mr. Babb, but it was Mr. Cohn's beginning comment as Mr. Babb entered his office a few days later that apparently headed off the expected tirade.

"Mr. Babb, you know I'll always listen to you, but I think

you ought to relax," he told the exasperated sales manager as he entered the room. Mr. Babb's attitude changed completely. He said his piece but in a respectful manner.

Mr. Cohn thanked him for the information and asked if he would like to stay with the company. Mr. Babb said he intended to resign and return to Champaign. This he did, buying a drive-in restaurant which became a big and loyal Continental customer.

Almost ten years later, Continental bought a company in Decatur, Illinois, not far from Champaign, and Mr. Babb called Stan Owens to say he had sold his restaurant and would like to return and work as a salesman out of the Decatur branch. Remembering his record as a salesman, Mr. Owens hired him, noting that if Mr. Babb had "burned his bridges" that day in Mr. Cohn's office, he couldn't have done so.

Meanwhile, the Glendale situation began to improve, and Continental began to make its way in the Los Angeles area. The private-label business was phased out in favor of increased foodservice, coffee and otherwise.

But the meager Glendale roasting capacity and its general shortage of space led the company to look for another facility. It found one in nearby Vernon, at 4650 Pacific Boulevard, where Huggins Young, a coffee-business competitor, vacated a plant and put it up for sale in late 1963.

Continental's building supervisor, Jim McManus, came out from Chicago to look it over. Even though it lacked roasting equipment, which Huggins Young had removed, he judged the plant suitable. Continental bought it and moved into it in December, 1963.

Charles McNichols, assistant superintendent in the Chicago plant, opened the new operation as its superintendent. Gene Sinser, an assistant to branch manager Simon Rice in New Jersey, was sent as branch manager. The German-born Mr. Sinser was a very thorough man who could be counted on to attend to the smallest necessary details.

Glendale was closed, and Frank Halsted, its very capable roaster, went to Vernon. The timing was just right, since the Glendale lease ran out about this time.

A few months after the Vernon plant was opened, that is, in March of 1964, Joe Harjung was sent from Chicago to help Mr. McNichols for three weeks. Then he returned to Chicago but came back in May to be warehouse manager at Vernon for the allied foods and equipment distribution in the Los Angeles area under Mr. McNichols, who was general superintendent. About three years later, Mr. McNichols died of a heart attack, and Mr. Harjung was made superintendent at Vernon.

Meanwhile, in September of 1964, Continental was approached by yet another seller, Folger Coffee Company, which had just been acquired by Procter & Gamble. Folger had a recently established institutional coffee business which the Federal Trade Commission was telling P&G it had to relinquish.

Continental bought this institutional business after being contacted by Folger as the company most qualified to take it over. Alvin and Robert Cohn and Stanley Owens flew to San Francisco to negotiate the purchase with the Folger people. The negotiations took all of seventy-five minutes.

Acquisition of the Folger business was a big boost for the Vernon operation. Folger stopped institutional roasting in San Francisco and Continental moved that roasting to Vernon. This gave Vernon a lot more to do. Indeed, the Vernon plant was to be the center of Continental's entire California coffee output.

With Folger came Jack Moore, who had started the institutional business for that company. As Folger's West Coast foodservice sales manager, Mr. Moore had a flair for expensive sales efforts. These included on one occasion renting a yacht and chef for ten days to bring Folger customers from Seattle to Los Angeles for a football game. He became West

Coast sales manager for Continental, practicing West Coast flamboyance in a manner with which Continental executives, especially Stanley Owens, were not entirely comfortable.

He sold accounts in Hawaii, for instance, which Stan Owens judged not worth the expense of monthly trips by Mr. Moore. So Mr. Owens cut the trips back to four times a year — a draconian measure about which Mr. Moore complained to Alvin Cohn. His complaint was to no avail, however.

Indeed, Mr. Owens finally disbanded the Continental sales force in Hawaii, turning over Continental distribution to Sunshine Distributors, headed by Harry Nita. Mr. Nita did good work on the islands. Once he worked accounts receivable up to a big $75,000 but explained that it was because customers were loading up in fear of a dock strike. He promised Continental would get it all back, and it did.

These acquisitions of the early 1960s were mere preliminary. The chains and national foodservice accounts were heading for areas of high and growing populations, and Continental's strategic planning pointed inevitably in the same direction. After the '60s came a deluge, a fair portion of it concentrated in California, where in five years Continental bought seven companies, of forty-one acquired nationwide in the same period.

The first of these California acquisitions, in 1970, was Goodrich & McWilliams, Inc., of Fresno, a distributor of frozen foods. Phil Goodrich, cleancut and articulate, fifty-eight years old, was the outside man, handling sales. Ernie McWilliams, fifty-five, handled the inside operation. Their sales manager was a big, strapping, outspoken fellow who could talk chefs' language and was very effective.

Mr. Goodrich's health was failing, and Mr. McWilliams feared his inability to buy the company in case of his partner's death or incapacitation. Paul Eibert, who had joined Continental in the '50s when his family's coffee business in Minneapolis was acquired by Continental, discovered the Goodrich & McWilliams opportunity. Years later the Goodrich & McWilliams operation was integrated into Continental's San Francisco business.

Another West Coast frozen-food operation bought in 1970 was Arctic Gardens/MG Frozen Foods, in Seattle and Tacoma, acquired as part of Continental's strategy of building on a strong coffee-route presence where possible — in this case in Seattle. In 1971 the Seattle-Tacoma combination was completed with the purchase of Standard Grocery Company, in Tacoma. More later about the integration of coffee-route, frozen-food and dry-groceries operations in this area.

The next California buy, also negotiated by Paul Eibert, was of Delaney Brothers Sea Food Company, in Newport Beach, in 1971. This was another mainly frozen-food operation, run by two brothers. One wanted out of the business. The other, Nick, an aggressive and intelligent man with a distinctive personality, stayed on after the Continental purchase.

In 1972 alone, Continental made three California-based acquisitions, one each in Vernon, San Diego and Los Angeles. The Vernon buy was of a distributor with about $15 million a year sales of dry groceries, paper goods, equipment and supplies — Kling Brothers & Fischer, Inc.

Art and Sig Kling had started their business in 1947 as wagon-jobbers, selling out of an army ambulance which they had bought from the Veterans Administration in San Diego. Sig had worked for S. E. Rykoff. Art had come to California after military service in Europe. The family had immigrated from Germany in the 1930s. Art had worked for a cousin in the restaurant business and then worked in neon signs before going into the army.

In due time the brothers had joined with Marvin Fischer, who with his wife had started his company in the back of a store. Along the way, the Klings bought up a number of wagon-jobbers — some more than once, since what they had bought were essentially customers. By 1972, with margins slim and a constant need for new capital, Sig Kling was ready to call it a career; and the three decided to let a buyer set the price which they would then divide among themselves.

The acquisition turned out for Continental to be the key to its growth in California, but at the last minute it almost didn't happen. Stan Owens and attorney Jerry Marks took over negotiations, which were moving slowly, when Paul Eibert left on a long-scheduled vacation.

The two met Art and Sig Kling, Marvin Fischer and Jerry Rabinowitz, their sales manager, in their attorney's office in Los Angeles. Mr. Fischer began calling for changes in the agreement previously struck with Paul Eibert, until Stanley Owens, irritated and beginning to wonder if he wanted the deal at all, finally told them to take or leave what he had on the table. It was 3:15 P.M. He and Mr. Marks were to catch a 5 P.M. plane for Chicago.

The two went to another room. Art Kling argued for accepting the Continental offer and prevailed. They called Mr. Owens and Mr. Marks back. Mr. Fischer asked, "Who's going to run the company?"

"You are," said Mr. Owens.

"It's a deal," said Mr. Fischer. Continental wired them the check the next day.

The three — Art Kling, Marv Fischer and Jerry Rabinowitz — ran the company out of their fine building in Vernon, continuing to make their business grow. The operation gave Continental its entree to the Los Angeles full-line market, where previously Continental had sold only coffee and specialty food items.

Six months later, Continental bought another Los Angeles-area distributor, Sunshine Specialty Products Company, based in Los Angeles itself. Sunshine was not as big as Kling Brothers & Fischer, but its volume was respectable, and it had carved a niche for itself in selling not only to restaurants and other away-from-home eating places but to smaller distributors as well.

The owners — Lou Wagman, Murray Wager and Nathan Schwartz — were all getting on in years and Messrs. Wager and Schwartz, already retired, wanted out of the business entirely. All three may have sensed in the Kling Brothers & Fischer sale a sign of their own diminished future as a small independent.

They contacted Mr. Eibert, and the sale was made. Mr. Wagman stayed on to run the Sunshine operation until the big integration of the four Los Angeles-area companies in 1975.

The four were Continental Coffee Company of California, now in Vernon, having moved there from Glendale when the facility grew too small; Delany Brothers, in Newport Beach; Kling Brothers & Fischer, also in Vernon; and Sunshine, in Los Angeles.

A common plant was needed. Glenn Tobin, Continental's man in charge of warehousing and distribution, and Stan Owens searched the area. Finally with the help of outside consultants, they settled on Vernon. Here the company put up a 210,00-square-foot building, its biggest facility to that time and since.

The new Vernon plant had loads of space, allocated this way: 144,000 square feet for dry goods, under an extra-high 32-foot ceiling; cooler-freezer space of 46,000 square feet; 20,000 square feet of office space—for a grand total of 210,000 square feet. It remains easily the biggest Continental plant.

Each of the four companies were moved into it one at a time. As this happened, their integration was begun as one new company. This was not a simple proposition. Frozen food salesmen from Delaney Brothers, for instance, didn't know the dry food business of Kling Brothers & Fischer, and vice versa. But Continental had always emphasized training for its salesmen and managers; so it was up to the challenge.

The third 1972 California acquisition was of a San Diego distributor, Palomar Foods Company. Palomar was distinguished for its manager, Donald Irwin, who was experienced and respected in the industry and had owned his own company for many years. But it was not distinguished for its facility, which was modest to the point of inadequacy. The facility so hampered the operation that after some difficult years the operation was merged with Los Angeles. Today San Diego-area orders are shipped out of Los Angeles.

Meanwhile, Continental's ongoing investigations of the industry showed them they had to increase their presence in its fastest-growing segment—fast-food/limited-menu restaurants. Much thought was given to the matter of how best to become involved. Naturally, the tilt was towards well-managed, respected suppliers with adequate facilities and a niche in the market.

Two acquisitions at this time filled the bill. One was a shortening-producer with a plant in Vernon, the other a California-based baking company. Together, they permitted Continental to begin much expanded service to the fast-food industry. The shortening-maker, Chicago-based Interstate Foods Corporation, acquired in 1972, had plants in Chicago and Vernon. Interstate in California is headed today by Joe Harjung.

The other purchase connected with fast-food service was of Freund Baking Company in 1973, with plants in City of Industry, near Los Angeles, and San Jose, near San Francisco. Freund baked buns for McDonald's exclusively. The company's two excellent, modern facilities were run by Harold Freund, a baking-industry veteran who had retired to California.

Mr. Freund had set up the two plants at McDonald's request. Continental, already doing coffee business with McDonald's, sounded McDonald's out about the Freund purchase. McDonald's had no objection but cautioned that the Freund buns should remain exclusively theirs. The acquisition gave

Continental a strong foothold in fast food — the highly specialized, fastest-growing segment of the foodservice industry.

Continental then, asked by Burger King and Wendy's to bake buns for them, set up the Orlando and Fresno bakeries, one right after the other. At Orlando buns were made in a state-of-the-art operation in a new building. At Fresno, they were made in smaller, rented quarters.

The California story cannot be told without special reference to the present head of Continental's sales and distribution division, Rich Seigel. Mr. Seigel has worked his entire Continental career on the West Coast, most of it in California. More than anyone else he is responsible for Continental's California success, primarily by his supervising the difficult, all-important integration of the four Los Angeles companies.

Mr. Seigel first worked for Continental in the specialty services division in Chicago during the summer of 1967, after his graduation from Knox College and before he started graduate school. In 1970, his MBA in hand from the Amos Tuck School of Business at Dartmouth, he made the California move he'd planned since childhood. It had become "almost an obsession" with him to live and work in that fabled state.

He took a job with Pacific Telephone, but by year's end had an interview with Stan Owens, who then headed Continental's sales and distribution division — later renamed foodservice division. Continental had just gone public.

The two met at the St. Francis Hotel, in San Francisco. Mr. Owens asked him to do something Mr. Seigel thought odd at the time but has since used as an interviewing technique, namely write a letter saying what he thought he could accomplish at Continental.

The letter made sense to Mr. Owens, and on April 1, 1971, Mr. Seigel went to work for Continental. His assignment was to coordinate consolidation of the three Seattle-area operations — Continental Coffee Company, Arctic Gardens/MG Frosted Foods and Standard Grocery — into one large facility.

The Seattle integration went smoothly. During its process Mr. Seigel was able to learn much from the three managers involved — Walter Struck, of Continental Coffee of Seattle; Larry Mattson, of Arctic Gardens, a frozen foods operation; and William Castro, of Standard (wholesale) Grocery.

He was anxious to return to California, however. So Stan Owens sent him to Vernon to work with Kling Brothers & Fischer. Consolidation of the Los Angeles plants was not far off, and Mr. Owens wanted to use Mr. Seigel's Seattle experience in this Los Angeles consolidation.

In due time Mr. Seigel and Marvin Fischer, Western area president, began planning the integration. But they disagreed on this process, and Mr. Seigel took a short leave of absence from the company. He returned to help Mr. Fischer again in the integration process, which he helped to conclude. In 1975 Mr. Owens sent Mr. Seigel to manage the San Diego branch, and he and his wife settled down in beautiful San Diego.

It was apparently the fulfillment of his dream. But the Los Angeles operation — that difficult consolidation in a difficult market — was in trouble. In March of 1978, Stan Owens offered Mr. Seigel the head job in Los Angeles, effective immediately.

He took it on one condition, that he be given enough authority to deal with a messy situation in which he knew he would have to contend with "turmoil, nepotism and shenanigans." Because of the consolidation of four companies, CFS Continental of California was not what Mr. Seigel considered a well disciplined company.

Off Mr. Seigel went to the city of angels, luckily with three years in San Diego behind him that gave him authority beyond what Stan Owens bestowed on him. It was the "quagmire" he had thought it would be, and he had to make changes. People didn't always like the changes, but they couldn't claim he didn't know the business, he said later.

He found some "very good people" already on the scene.

But he still moved people about, giving some more responsibility, showing others the door, changing systems and procedures. Most important, he feels (and others agree with him) that he played it straight with everybody, going behind no one's back, encouraging in all things a team effort.

It helped that he was identified with neither of the four companies. More important was that he had "walked in the shoes" of the people he was leading. He hadn't moved in from a different business.

He himself promoted from within. Today he looks fondly on the "loyalties of forty-five years ago" when Stan Owens began with Continental Coffee Company. He embraces for himself the goal of encouraging such loyalty. To do this he knows he can't fool people. He believes in putting good people in charge and giving them authority. "If you interfere, you give them an excuse," he says.

Aaron Clark, Los Angeles-based financial advisor to the Cohns and to CFS Continental, witnesses to Rich Seigel's intentions to build an organization. When Mr. Seigel arrived in Los Angeles, Mr. Clark called and offered him entree to some major customers. It was a tempting offer, made by someone who wanted to help, but Mr. Seigel refused. He was there to build an organization, he told Mr. Clark, and being served customers on a silver platter was no way to do it.

By March, 1983, not only was Los Angeles under Mr. Seigel's supervision, but so were Fresno, Reno, Phoenix and Billings, where Continental had gotten its start in full-line distribution. In that month Alvin Cohn asked him to take a newly created position, executive vice-president of sales and distribution (later foodservice). He answered with a question: what was the difference between that and being president of S&D?

Mr. Cohn was taken aback by the question, which Mr. Seigel posed by way of pressing the issue of full responsibility. Mr. Cohn said that if Mr. Seigel's record warranted it, he would be made president of S&D. This did happen, and Mr. Seigel remains in that position.

S&D headquarters, previously in Chicago, simply went with its president to Los Angeles. The division absorbed national purchasing and created its own control function. Some key national account maintenance has been located with the division. Mr. Seigel intends to complete staff formation so that it can meet the responsibilities he envisions for it.

Twenty-five years after Frank Hoffmann began selling Continental coffee in Los Angeles, therefore, a major division of CFS Continental is headquartered in that city, and business is better than ever.

Another part of the California story is establishment in the early 1970s of Continental's buying office — part of the great shift away from being a coffee company to becoming a full-service supplier of institutional food outlets.

As a wholesaler to a major industry, Continental was under pressure to make itself as efficient as possible. Management looked to more efficient ways to do its buying and pass on the savings to customers. The buying office represented a major move in that direction.

Its origins coincided with the hiring in 1972 of Earl Heitger, former divisional president with Consolidated Foods and more recently head of institutional foods for Swift. Mr. Heitger was hired by Stan Owens to head a new corporate buying office and take over the entire Continental marketing effort.

Continental at the time was using a broker in San Francisco for its West Coast buying. The broker consolidated orders from the various Continental distribution centers. This was a common arrangement in the industry.

Messrs. Heitger and Owens both felt there had to be a better way to do the buying. They set up a committee to consider alternatives. The committee was to consist of people from operations and others who knew food buying. These were chosen: Billy Meyers from Indianapolis, Jack Leppert from Detroit, Dick Stultz from Billings, and Mr. Heitger. The committee met several times. The San Francisco broker joined one of the sessions. The committee ended up unanimously recommending that Continental establish its own buying office in Los Angeles.

When word got out about the decision, Michael Bearman called Stan Owens and volunteered to head it up. Mr. Bearman had joined Continental when his firm, United Food Service Supply Company, in St. Paul, was acquired by Continental. With Harold Neifeld he had built United Food Service, spending his time mostly in purchasing for that firm. He also had spent a good deal of time with customers; so he could be expected to understand their problems.

In support of his candidacy for the position, Mr. Bearman pointed out that his wife was a UCLA graduate and was anxious to return to Los Angeles. Mr. Bearman received the assignment and went to Los Angeles, where he rented office space and began hiring staff. At that point Alvin Cohn suggested they invite the West Coast suppliers to lunch as a way of introducing themselves.

Invitations went out and the luncheon was held at the Fairmont Hotel in San Francisco, with 100 percent attendance by the suppliers. It was the first time that buyers took suppliers to lunch. Usually it was the other way around. But the Continental people wanted the suppliers to know theirs was a quality house and would insist on quality to match the Continental label.

As far as price went, Continental expected to pay a fair price though not always the lowest. The luncheon did serve to introduce Continental to the suppliers. In fact, a brief greeting to them by Alvin Cohn and Stan Owens elicited a standing ovation, and many came up afterwards to say how much they appreciated the gesture.

Mickey Bearman took over the buying office. For his staff he hired several women with West Coast buying experience. The office grew with the company. In 1976 Mr. Bearman was joined by Art Kling, whose firm Kling Brothers & Fischer had been acquired in 1972.

There had been a good deal of change in the Los Angeles distribution center since the big consolidation. Mr. Kling's responsibilities had been slowly merged with others'. But his expertise in imported food items remained unique.

At the same time, the buying office in Los Angeles was not giving enough attention to purchase of imported items. So Mr. Kling was offered a position in the buying office handling imported items exclusively. He came to the task with extensive experience as a buyer, accustomed to going overseas when necessary for quality and price. Others assumed foreign buying was only for specialty, high markup items, but Mr. Kling knew better.

For Continental, as for Kling Brothers & Fischer, Mr. Kling shopped overseas for tuna, olives, asparagus, mushrooms, artichokes, pimientos, pineapples and anything else that was grown well and sold at reasonable prices. He knew how it worked. Asparagus in Formosa, for instance, was packed by hand and was picked by stoop labor. Such stoop labor was no longer being performed in the U. S., because of restrictions on use of Mexican nationals as farm workers. Low production costs overseas made low prices possible here at no lessening of quality.

Or the foreign-bought product simply gave better value. For instance, Kling Brothers & Fischer bought Japanese tuna because it was packed in less water. On the street this was a selling point: tuna carrying the Kling Brothers (later Continental) label offered more drained weight.

Mr. Kling bought Mexican pineapple, then Formosan pineapple and Malaysian paprika and pineapple for Kling Brothers, following the market for best buys. Malaysian (crushed) pineapple, much in demand for cooking, was a good buy because it came in more tightly packed quantities.

He continued these practices for the Continental buying office over a four-year period ending January of 1980. When he came in January of 1976, Continental was buying olives in 5-case lots from a Los Angeles warehouse. He bought them in Spain in 850-case containers at big savings.

He did the same with artichokes, pimientos, pineapple and anything else he could get better and cheaper. He stayed alert to what he was getting, of course. When he received a shipment of "Hawaiian pineapple" from the Philippines, he threatened to send it back. The seller reduced the price and from then on there were two kinds of Hawaiian pineapple — from Hawaii and from the Philippines — labeled that way so the buyers knew what they were getting.

The results of Mr. Kling's new buying practices became clear. In the first Lenten tuna promotion following his arrival at the buying office, the company sold 25,000 cases. When it came to mushrooms, Minneapolis buyer Tom Stenger went from almost no sales to 85 cases every three weeks.

There was selling to do within the company, however, because of the wrong impression many had that foreign-bought items were more expensive. Mr. Kling sang his "lowest price on the street" tune to Continental salesmen and branch managers from Seattle to Florida and New Jersey to San Diego in efforts to ween them, old and new, away from their prejudice against foreign-bought goods.

Some of his own tried-and-true practices helped. He followed the rule, for instance, that he would cut losses early when stuck with something that was not selling, no matter where it had been bought. He would cut prices to move what was not moving, even if it meant a loss. Better that than lose the whole amount. "First loss is best," he says.

Mr. Kling had bypass surgery in April of 1979 and retired on January 1, 1980.

The buying office later moved nomad-like across the country — from Los Angeles to Stockton (near San Francisco), to Chicago and then back to Los Angeles. Purchasing became more sophisticated in the 1980s, thanks largely to computer-supplied access to information about markets and suppliers. Even more important became the access to branch inventories by which the buying office monitors the movement of merchandise and the stocks on hand. This information is especially helpful when a supplier offers a "special" and the decision to buy must be made right away.

The buying office also buys more for the branches than it once did — items not bought at all before (fresh meat, for instance) and items previously bought by the branches. And the buyers fan out from California to the branches for regular visits, the better to coordinate their efforts with those of the branch purchasing departments.

14. GOING PUBLIC AND WHAT FOLLOWED

The possibility of going public was put to Jacob Cohn as early as the 1950s. Ben Regan, former co-owner of Nationwide Food Service and a friend of Alvin Cohn, urged this course on him. Mr. Regan, a securities salesman for Hornblower & Weeks, had worked with Todd Ebers in running Nationwide Food Service, which sold mostly to industrial cafeterias. The two had sold Nationwide to Canteen Corporation.

Mr. Regan, a big, good-looking fellow and a good salesman, met his match in Jacob Cohn, even if he was a friend of Mr. Cohn's son.

"I don't want to worry about stockholders at the expense of customers," said Mr. Cohn, and the case was closed.

Meanwhile, the Cohns and Stanley Owens felt the need to solve a more pressing problem, how to protect Jacob Cohn's survivors from heavy inheritance taxes. Mr. Cohn was by far the biggest shareowner, and the company's value was considerable. In the 1950s Continental was selling more coffee to the foodservice industry than General Foods or Standard Brands, previous leaders in foodservice coffee sales.

If it were publicly held, the market would set a price. But because it was privately held, its value at Mr. Cohn's death would be for lawyers to decide, and the government would be sure to investigate this decision very carefully. The solution was to reorganize the corporation, creating preferred stock for Mr. Cohn and transferring his common stock to his family.

With common stock comes control of the company. But in this case, a special condition was laid down, that if the company paid no preferred dividends for eight quarters, Jacob Cohn would take back control of the company. This never happened. His sons thus took control of the company five years or so before his death.

In 1967, as we have seen, they were approached by Super Valu, the huge Minneapolis-based wholesale grocery company, which would have bought Continental in effect to run its small foodservice division, called Harrison House. This deal did not materialize, though Robert Cohn initially liked the idea as an alternative to going public.

The challenge remained how to achieve growth by acquisition, which was their chosen strategy. The company needed a medium of exchange for its growth. Publicly traded stock would be this medium. But Jacob Cohn was lukewarm to the idea of having the public own shares of his company.

Some months after his death in June of 1968, Continental began to address questions connected with going public. Involved in this process were the company's auditors, Price Waterhouse, and Louis Leichentritt, Continental's vice-president-finance and treasurer.

Mr. Leichentritt, who died suddenly while this book was being prepared, had joined Continental in 1947 as a college student on the G.I. bill. The company answered an ad he placed in the *Chicago Tribune* for part-time work and put him in the credit department at ninety cents an hour. Later he became the company's first Certified Public Accountant.

He was in a position to see the work of another who helped the company work its way through the process of going public, namely former U. S. Supreme Court Justice Abe Fortas. Howard Koven, Continental's chief lawyer, gained the services of Mr. Fortas, who would sit in on meetings saying nothing for long periods and then speak for a half hour showing he'd been listening and taking everything in.

Loeb Rhoades handled the stock issue. Private shareholders as usual were given the opportunity to sell. The biggest amount realized from the sale was to go to the company treasury. But in six months or so, the company felt Loeb Rhoades was not energetic enough in selling the stock.

This is when Aaron Clark, Los Angeles-based financial advisor to the Cohns, suggested (when asked) that they talk to his brother Phil, a senior partner at Drexel Burnham. They did, and Phil Clark did much to increase public awareness of Continental. As a result, Continental drew close to Drexel Burnham.

Meanwhile, Continental's newly acquired status as a public company led to an increase in the number of directors, not for window dressing but to give needed advice and direction.

These outside directors would supplement guidance provided for decades by the Cohn brothers and Stanley Owens. Alvin Cohn was chairman of the board, having succeeded his late father in that position. Robert Cohn was still president.

The new directors had to be of good business reputation and able to relate to a company led and largely owned by two brothers. They could not be with a company from which Continental might get a lot of business.

Charles W. Lubin, founder of The Kitchens of Sara Lee, and James R. Kennedy, vice-chairman of the Celanese Corporation, were the first. They joined the board in 1971. Solomon Dutka, president and later chairman of Audits and Surveys, Inc., joined the following year, 1972, recommended by Aaron Clark.

In 1974, Harold Freund, chairman of the newly acquired Harold Freund Baking Company, became a director. Mr. Owens became vice-chairman. Howard Koven, the company's attorney for more than twenty-five years, joined in 1976; Walter B. Scott, vice-president and director of Motorola, the following year. In 1978 there were two new directors, Walter G. Gadient, vice-president and director of Lincoln National

Corporation, and Thomas F. Wands, senior vice-president-operations and director of Sears Roebuck & Company.

Mr. Lubin became director emeritus in 1980. Robert Burgin, chairman and chief executive of Leaseway Transportation Corporation, took his place.

In 1983 Donald Hansen, who had come to CFS Continental from W. W. Grainger, Inc., two years earlier as executive vice-president-administration, became the last board member to be elected before the Staley merger. Mr. Hansen had been executive vice-president and a director at W. W. Grainger, where he had been involved with distribution, warehousing and data processing. At Continental he assumed responsibility for these functions and several administrative areas. Later he also became responsible for Continental's manufacturing divisions nationwide.

Most of these directors were obtained by Robert Cohn, who picked them for a variety of skills. Mr. Scott, for instance, was especially noted for his experience with participatory management. Recommendations counted, of course. Alvin Cohn, seeking the chairman of Sears Roebuck, was referred to Mr. Wands, who later recommended Mr. Burgin.

Another effect of going public was to enable the company to reward its managers with stock options. This did much to mold them into a team. It was an application of an old Jacob Cohn principal of providing incentives by giving people a share in the gains. Such arrangements encourage people to see their own prosperity entwined with the company's.

In 1973 the company changed its name to CFS Continental. It was partly a problem of image. This was "more than a coffee company," as its trade advertising was saying. And it was much less a coffee company than ever. Coffee was twenty-five percent of sales. In a few years it would be less than sixteen percent.

There was also the problem raised by both lawyers and accountants, who said the name had to be changed because the company was no longer selling enough coffee to justify it.

A "Dear Fellow Employee" letter from Alvin and Robert Cohn on April 17, 1973, said the new name reflected the company's "broader range" of activities. The company had "constantly adapted" to changing markets since it was founded fifty-eight years earlier, the brothers said. "Perhaps the most significant" change had begun about five years earlier with "a broad expansion of products and services" to the growing away-from-home foodservice industry.

Explanations vary for the choice of CFS Continental. Continental Foods would have been a natural, but it was ruled out because the company could not regain rights to its use. This name had been sold some decades earlier, when Lipton Tea had bought it with a dry soup mix bearing that name.

CFS stood for "coffee, foods and services," the company newsletter said. It might also have stood for Complete Food Service. No big issue was made of it. The important thing was to keep the well-known Continental name, but not all of it. The new CFS Continental was marketing products in eighty-two of the eighty-eight biggest U. S. metropolitan areas in the U. S. through thirty distribution centers.

Abe Fortas helped the company weather another crisis of sorts in 1974, when he cut through red tape and enabled it to plead its case for a price increase in the face of recently imposed wage-price controls. Mr. Leichentritt can still recall the look on the face of the young man in the appropriate Washington bureau when he was visited by Mr. Fortas and properly awed by him.

In 1975 Continental had no trouble finding investors for its first long-term debt-financing, of $40 million over twenty years, at 9¼%. Four days after putting the idea to ten insurance companies, eight companies chose to participate. The five who were chosen came in with checks totalling $6.5 million over the determined amount. They had to hurry and redo their checks, Mr. Leichentritt recalls.

With being public came the necessity of dealing with stock market analysts — a task that Mr. Leichentritt and later Stanley Owens assumed with enthusiasm. For Mr. Owens it was yet another role in his long Continental career, and one he relished.

The challenge Mr. Leichentritt and he faced was that the company, though well managed and growing in a growth industry, was not well known among stock analysts. "Continental who?" they asked when first approached. This was a company well known within a certain industry but not in the nation's households. Not even in its brokerage offices, for that matter.

As Continental grew, Mr. Leichentritt acquired increased responsibilities, including the responsibility for acquisitions; and he gradually withdrew from investor relations. Stanley Owens, who took on increased responsibilities in this area, approached the task with relish. He didn't doubletalk, was always ready to admit problems and was willing to tell an analyst he did not know an answer but would find out and let the analyst know. This latter was extremely important, because people do not like to be led on, stock market analysts least of all. He told them what he knew about the company, not what he hoped would happen.

Mr. Owens therefore added investor relations to his other tasks for Continental over the years. With investor relations, from the middle or late 1970s, Mr. Owens acquired another job, the coordination of annual reports. He was responsible for the first use of pictures in a Continental annual report. He was not about to present the Continental story in a dry and lifeless manner.

The results have been well received within both design and investor relations communities. The 1981 report won the Potlatch award of excellence for craftsmanship and creativity in graphic communications.

The 1982 report, designed by Gene Bellini, was the first of

several to feature on its cover a master work of art with a dining-out motif. This report won the Nicholson award given by the National Association of Investment Clubs (NAIC) as best for individual investors in the food industry and was furthermore rated in the top five reports overall.

The 1984 report, designed for Continental by Steven Bagby, won the Nicholson award too. This report also won in a juried decision the design excellence award of the Illinois Society of Typographical Artists.

Any success achieved with Continental's annual reports in the '80s must be attributed in part to Mitchell Saranow, vice-president and chief financial officer; Michael Urbut, vice-president and controller; and Brian Nocco, treasurer. Later, after Continental was acquired by Staley, Mr. Urbut's experience and abilities were recognized when he was made vice-president and controller of the new holding company, Staley-Continental.

Financial results tell the story — sales up from $193 million to $1.4 billion in fourteen years (1971 through 1984), net income from $4 million to $19.6 million. In 1973 and 1974, sales rose 27% and 25% respectively.

The 1974 report spoke of CFS Continental as "architects of distribution systems" and "foodservicers to the nation." Golden Bear Restaurants during the year were featured in ads saying they got "decor, dinnerware, detergents and desserts" from Continental. Luther College, Decorah, Iowa, got "lettuce, ladles, lamb and Ludefisk," the latter for some of its Norwegian staff. Dayton Hudson Corporation, Minneapolis, got "poultry, produce, paper and pickles," not to mention a "full-service equipment and supply program" for kitchen and dining-room tableware — "practically everything you need."

In 1975 the company announced its transformation from a coffee company to a major manufacturing and service organization with 70,000 customers in forty-three states.

A new consolidated distribution center had opened in Seattle, and the Chicago coffee roasting operation was moved to Houston, sixty years after Jacob Cohn began selling from his horsedrawn wagon.

In Los Angeles the company's largest plant under one roof, with 210,000 square feet, became operational in August of that year. Later in the year the Rosemont (Ill.) facility opened, near Chicago's O'Hare airport.

Revenues had quintupled, net income had tripled in ten years. Earnings per share had risen from 29¢ to $1, book value per share from $1.43 to $7.25, having risen steadily at 13%-to-15% each year.

The 1977 report told the bad news of the coffee-price explosion that shocked the industry and set Continental back for its first year in which earnings did not improve. Net income dropped to $2.1 million from $8.7 million, per-share income to 22¢ from $1.09. In the fourth quarter, Continental stock dropped to 5⅔, down from a second-quarter, 1976, high of 12.08.

But in 1978, a year of recovery, net income more than doubled, rising to $5.4 million; and earnings per share almost tripled, rising to 61¢. By 1982, earnings per share were $1.71.

Comments by the investment community shed light on the recent history of CFS Continental. In July of 1976, CFS could boast a constant stream of quarters in which higher earnings were recorded — "despite problems some others had," noted Smith Barney, Harris Upham & Co.

Trouble was coming, however — the great coffee price rise and decline of 1977, which sent shivers through the coffee industry. A freak frost in 1975 in Brazil, the world's leading coffee producer, set the stage. The resulting shortage was apparently seized on by Brazilian producers, who "essentially" withheld coffee to keep prices up, according to a November, 1977, Smith Barney report.

Caught in the middle were hundreds of suppliers, including Continental, whose people counted on coffee for a good chunk of its operating profits. Prices shot up, reaching $3.35 a pound for green coffee at their peak in April, up from $1.50. a pound seven months earlier, the Smith Barney report said. Industry veterans, for whom a nickel-a-pound raise was unusual, shook their heads.

The scenario was "particularly unfortunate" for Continental, said Smith Barney, because Continental had for a number of years been "successfully lessening the importance of coffee in its overall operations." From 34% of total revenue in 1970, coffee sales had dropped to 19% in 1976, as Continental developed "the concept of a full-line foodservice distributor."

But CFS Continental "expensed everything it could" in the fourth quarter, said the EGT (Eppler, Guerin, Turner) memorandum in June of 1978. As a result, the company took a fourth quarter 1977 loss and for the year reported a drop in earnings per share to 22¢, from $1.09 for the year before (restated).

A year later, in July of 1979, EGT reported continuing problems, however: coffee was still 15% of revenues but 30% of profits. Growth was possibly slowing in the restaurant and fast-food business, from which came 73% of corporate revenue. Chains, which accounted for 35% or more of business, were tight-margin customers who emphasized price over service.

On the plus side, some problem branches, once their problems were solved, held promise of increased earnings. Furthermore, the fragmented foodservice industry was ripe for the winning by companies that knew what they were doing and had the resources to do it. And Continental's stock was underpriced, in EGT's opinion.

Continental, now called CFS for short, was distributing some 7,000 items through twenty-seven service centers in thirty-nine states, including 97 of the 108 biggest metropolitan areas in the U. S. Forty percent of what the company distributed, it processed in its fourteen manufacturing centers.

As for the risk of another coffee "catastrophe," as another analyst called it, chances were much less of that happening again. Inventories were being held down and consumption patterns were being closely monitored. And CFS no longer participated in the 30-day price-protection programs that had contributed to its problems in 1977.

Now "quantum leaps" in coffee prices, which seemed unlikely, could be passed on immediately to customers, Blunt Ellis and Loewi observed in February of 1980. In addition, coffee was down to 11% of total volume. But Blunt Ellis had better things to talk about than that, namely the "marked improvement" Continental was achieving in handling its inventory and receivables.

Continental achieved this improvement — in an industry where inventory and receivables were both normally hefty — mainly through improved computerized purchasing and inventory-control systems. The company also had "increased depth in middle management." CFS had doubled its sales in five years while increasing its total debt by only 8%. "In effect," said Blunt Ellis, this was "self-financed growth."

Furthermore, the away-from-home market was showing consistent growth. Of the $50-billion foodservice industry, CFS, second largest in the industry, had only a 1.4% share. CFS had lots of room to grow in. The trend was still strong to multiline distribution at the expense of wholesalers who could not deliver so much over so wide an area. Further acquisitions were therefore possible. CFS, Blunt Ellis concluded, is a "very service-oriented company."

The company's ads in industry magazines emphasized service. A customer service rep in Atlanta, a truck driver in Eau Clair and a salesman in Grand Rapids were some of those featured. The Atlanta woman delivered pepperoni on her way home from work to a pizzamaker who saw he'd soon be out of the much-used item.

The driver in Eau Clair took a customer's frozen meats into

his freezer truck in the aftermath of a tornado that cut the town's power and put the customer's freezer out of commission. The Grand Rapids salesman interrupted Christmas with his family to run over to a doughnut shop and fix its coffeemaker.

CFS, said Bear Sterns in October of 1980, was a "highly attractive investment." Besides being big and well-organized in a "fragmented industry, the company had taken steps to improve its efficiency, closing or consolidating low-profit facilities. The Chicago (Rosemont) facility, however, was a problem, partly because of the depressed Midwest market which it served.

CFS common stock was "an outstanding value," in the view of Rotan Mosle, Inc., who in June of 1981 cited increasing professionalization of Continental management. This increase in professionalism showed itself in improved financial controls and pricing practices and in the management of major assets, receivables and inventories.

Coffee was 11% of revenues and 25% of profits. The Rosemont center still was not generating an adequate return, but its drain on profits was decreasing. The analyst noted the purchase, in progress at the time, of one of CFS's former Chicago-area competitors, Monarch's foodservice division, and said (accurately, as matters developed) that its addition should help Rosemont.

Six months later, in December of 1981, Smith Barney noted record sales and earnings for fiscal 1981 — $930 million, up 14%, and $1.41 (restated) a share, up 33%. Fourth-quarter sales had been up much more than that (30%), thanks in part to the Avard-Garth acquisition in the important Northern California market and the more recent Monarch-Chicago acquisition.

Favorable comments cropped up frequently in these years about CFS's strong orientation to the fast-growing fast-food industry (29% of sales in 1982) and the process of industry consolidation that so favored industry leaders such as CFS Continental.

There was frequent mention also of CFS's new bakeries in Fresno and Orlando, both serving fast-food outlets. They were at breakeven or better by February of 1984, said the Gill Report. Not quite, said First Boston Research, naming only Fresno, but they were both expected to do so in the next quarter.

This Fresno did, earning a slight profit, First Boston reported three months later. Indeed, the two bakeries together were expected to make a "modest earnings contribution" to fiscal 1984. The bakery division's problems were "apparently" solved, First Boston said.

Neither of the two bakeries were running near capacity a month later, in June of 1984, according to Value Line, but their futures looked bright. Two months later, First Boston was announcing a "turnaround" at the bakeries.

Coffee was still the biggest single product line, contributing not quite 20% of earnings in 1984, down from 40% in the mid-'70s. This decrease in dependence on coffee lessened the possibility of repeating the 1977 trouble, as did a recent International Coffee Organization agreement.

CFS was in a position to supply 80% to 85% of a customer's needs, everything but dairy products, Value Line reported in mid-'84. Its fast-food business was better than ever, with seven warehouses working to supply this industry's special needs, which included frequent deliveries at odd hours. CFS was gaining market share in this industry.

Virtually all of these analysts made "buy" recommendations. One short-term "buy" was changed to a "hold" because of recent rises in CFS's stock value and recent interest in food industry stocks in general. But even that was changed to "buy" for intermediate and long-term investors. And that same month, another analyst stayed with "buy" across the board.

The analysts liked CFS Continental. But it was First Boston who, in August of 1984, called attention to CFS's attractiveness to large diversified food companies seeking growth in the foodservice industry. These companies, said First Boston "may find CFS Continental an appropriate and worthwhile acquisition."

Not one but two of them did, both headquartered in Illinois. First Dart & Kraft, Inc., of Northbrook, and then A. E. Staley Manufacturing Company, of Decatur, found CFS attractive as an acquisition. In October of 1984, Staley paid $353.6 million, or $38 a share, for CFS.

As a $2.1-billion-sales food producer, Staley wanted to buffer the effects of commodity price fluctuations and participate in the growth of the foodservice industry. CFS, with $1.4 billion in 1984 sales, distributed some of what Staley made, such as condiments and food ingredients, and thus a match was possible.

CFS was attractive also because of its sophistication in data processing. The company's foodservice distribution and its manufacturing both benefited from timely, easily analyzed computer-fed information. Progress in this vital data-processing area was not new for Continental, as we have seen. Historically it enjoyed a number of computer firsts in foodservice, including its introduction some years earlier of Management Information Services (MIS) which in effect put the computer at the service of all CFS managers.

Another plus for Staley was CFS's strategic planning procedures — for almost twenty years a valuable tool in the hands of its leadership. CFS's strategic planning was admittedly not unique, but it had been notably successful in producing a regularly updated analysis and overview of foodservice and its components.

Finally, CFS enjoyed strong and happy relationships in the banking community and in general was highly respected in the financial community. Financial analysts, as we have seen, looked on CFS Continental as a strong, reliable performer.

After acquiring CFS, Staley management created a holding company, Staley Continental, and placed Robert Cohn and Alvin Cohn on its board of directors. CFS continued to enjoy operational autonomy, while the holding company provided financial and other corporate services. Expectations remained high that CFS would continue to show good growth in sales and earnings through its acquisitions, additions to its product line and growth in its established markets.

It was all as Jacob Cohn had intended it to be — not in its details, which he could not have imagined, but in its essence and in overall quality. What Mr. Cohn had begun in 1915 was in 1986, when this was being written, stronger than ever.

Jim Bowman is author of *Booz, Allen & Hamilton, Seventy Years of Client Service: 1914–1984*. A former reporter for the *Chicago Daily News* and former columnist for the *Chicago Tribune,* he writes company histories and other business-oriented materials from his home in Oak Park, Illinois.